"This Poetick Liturgie"

For Jan, Jason and Joel

A. LEIGH DENEEF

"*This Poetick Liturgie*"

ROBERT HERRICK'S
CEREMONIAL
MODE

Durham, North Carolina

DUKE UNIVERSITY PRESS

1974

PR
3512
H43
D4

PRINTED IN THE UNITED STATES OF
AMERICA BY HERITAGE PRINTERS

CONTENTS

ACKNOWLEDGMENTS

I SHOULD LIKE to express appreciation for the professional help and encouragement of my friends, colleagues, and former teachers. Ralph W. Condee, Elmer Borklund, Peter Skutches, Louis A. Haselmayer, and Edmund Reiss all offered useful advice. The anonymous Press readers have helped me more than I can adequately repay. My greatest debts are to Ralph Condee, whose early and continuing guidance and friendship served to stimulate my better efforts and to curb my weaker ones. Ashbel Brice and John Menapace helped prepare the book for the press.

The Duke University Research Council provided a grant to assist in the publication of this manuscript, for which I am grateful. The staffs of the Pennsylvania State University Library and the Duke University Library also deserve my thanks for their kind assistance.

Permission to quote from *The Complete Poetry of Robert Herrick*, edited by J. Max Patrick, was graciously extended by Doubleday & Company. I am grateful as well to the editors of the *South Atlantic Quarterly, Renaissance Papers, Notes and Queries,* and *Seventeenth-Century News* for permission to reprint material which appeared first in their journals.

Finally, I wish to acknowledge the persistent encouragement of my wife, who has read, typed, and questioned virtually every page of this study and without whose help it could never have been done.

"This Poetick Liturgie"

CHAPTER I

THE CEREMONIAL MODE

IN THE FIRST book-length study of Robert Herrick, published in 1910, F. W. Moorman remarked in passing: "Herrick's allusions to these ceremonial rites [involving pagan "household" deities] are so simple and so intimate that they give to his verses something more than a merely antiquarian colour."[1] Some fifty years later, in the second edition of *English Literature in the Earlier Seventeenth Century*, Douglas Bush echoed Moorman's hint: "Herrick's attitude is refined and deepened by his instinct for ceremonial, in life and in art."[2] Both statements express a long-standing feeling readers have had about some sort of festive, ritualizing process at work in the *Hesperides*, and they have been repeated frequently in later scholarship.[3] The first systematic attempt to define that ceremonial process, though, was not until 1955 with Thomas R. Whitaker's "Herrick and the Fruits of the Garden," which begins by asserting that "Herrick colors all with a feeling for *art*—the subtle crafts of feminine adornment, poetry, and ritual. This last is especially important, for, as the opening verses [of the *Hesperides*] make clear, this is above all a ceremonial poetry."[4] Taking "The Funeral Rites of the Rose" as his seminal example, Whitaker demonstrates how Herrick constructs "religious" rites in order to transcend the fact of death in several of his burial poems. More recently, Robert H. Deming, in a dissertation on "The Classical Ceremonial in the Poetry of Robert Herrick," extended the limits of Whitaker's

1. Moorman, *Robert Herrick* (London, 1910), p. 206.
2. Bush, *English Literature in the Earlier Seventeenth Century*, 2nd ed. (Oxford, 1962), pp. 116–17.
3. Earl Miner's provocative references to ceremony throughout *The Cavalier Mode from Jonson to Cotton* (Princeton, 1971) are the most recent examples.
4. Whitaker, "Herrick and the Fruits of the Garden," *English Literary History* 22 (1955): 17.

analysis by locating and defining the various historical rites Herrick alludes to or reproduces in all the poems.[5]

The studies of Whitaker and Deming have contributed significantly to Herrick scholarship by defining aspects of the poet's use of ritual, and together they have made it now possible to see that Herrick's artistic process throughout the volume is controlled by a conscious *poetic* ceremonial. By *poetic* ceremonial, I mean not merely Herrick's use of classical rites in certain burial poems, but the mode of poetic expression shaping individual lyrics within, and perhaps the whole of, the *Hesperides*—understanding here by "mode of expression," "a way of interpreting experience, a measure of ordering that experience and giving it conspicuous artistic form."[6] In the most general terms, the method of such a ceremonial mode is to isolate specific and limited instants of human experience and to transform them into significant and static celebratory rites in which both poet and reader participate. By understanding the nature of these *poetic* rites and the artistic consciousness shaping them, it is possible to gain a clearer perspective on Herrick's intents and achievement.

Some general hypotheses concerning the ceremonial mode can be established by analyzing Herrick's "The Argument of his Book" (H-1).[7] Since the "Argument" introduces the *Hesperides*, it can be assumed that the poem presents the major speaking voice, or persona, the poet will adopt in the volume as a whole. The qualification here of "major" voice is essential because too frequently discussions of Herrick have emphasized individual dramatic speakers rather than the conscious variety of voices adopted.[8] The problem is that despite

5. Deming, "The Classical Ceremonial," Diss. Univ. of Wisconsin, 1956; and "Robert Herrick's Classical Ceremonial," *English Literary History* 34 (1967): 327–48.

6. Donald M. Friedman, *Marvell's Pastoral Art* (Berkeley, 1970), p. 7.

7. All citations of Herrick's verse are taken from *The Complete Poetry of Robert Herrick*, ed. J. Max Patrick (New York, 1963), and the numbering of poems from both the *Hesperides* and the *Noble Numbers* follows this edition.

8. Roger B. Rollin's *Robert Herrick* (New York, 1966) sees Herrick's volume as unified by a consistently pastoral persona; Floris Delattre's *Robert Herrick* (Paris, 1912) argues the same unity by virtue of a courtly Cavalier persona. Herrick's "Roman" voice is defined most fully by Pauline Aiken, "The Influence of the Latin Elegists on English Lyric Poetry, 1600–1650," *University of Maine*

the invaluable information such discussions provide about Herrick's pastoral, courtly, realistic (epigrammatic), or artistic persona,[9] they do not show that all the speakers, regardless of their individual subjects and concerns, are united by a common attitude. That all four personae engage in essentially the same act of ritualistic celebration clarifies Herrick's commitment to a ceremonial mode of poetry.

The initial words of "The Argument," then, identify its persona as a singer: "I Sing of . . ." "Singing" is, of course, the traditional function of a number of generic voices: the epic narrator, the Old English scop, the romance minstrel, the Renaissance sonneteer, the seventeenth-century Cavalier lyricist. Of more importance is the fact that for the lyric voice to "sing" a subject is to celebrate and praise that subject, to raise or elevate it to a level of significance greater than it would normally have. As George T. Wright suggests, the act of "singing" brooks, blossoms, birds, and bowers is itself an assertion of their ultimate value.[10]

> I Sing of *Brooks*, of *Blossomes*, *Birds*, and *Bowers*:
> Of *April*, *May*, of *June*, and *July*-Flowers.
> I sing of *May-poles*, *Hock-carts*, *Wassails*, *Wakes*,
> Of *Bride-grooms*, *Brides*, and of their *Bridall-cakes*.
> I write of *Youth*, of *Love*, and have Accesse
> By these, to sing of cleanly-*Wantonnesse*.
> I sing of *Dewes*, of *Raines*, and piece by piece

Studies, 2nd Series, 22 (1932), and by Kathryn A. McEuen, *Classical Influence upon the Tribe of Ben* (Cedar Rapids, 1939). Richard Ross, in a 1958 University of Michigan dissertation entitled " 'A Wilde Civilitie': Robert Herrick's Poetic Solution of the Paradox of Art and Nature," and John L. Kimmey, in "Robert Herrick's Persona," *Studies in Philology* 67 (1970): 221–36, argue for a specifically "poetic" persona.

9. Although these four personae will be defined in succeeding chapters, a note of caution may be sounded here: I am not insisting that these are the only identifiable voices in the *Hesperides* or that they are always distinguishable from each other; indeed, there may be some overlapping, as in "To Dean-bourn" (H–86). Nonetheless, the four do seem to be the major personae Herrick uses with some degree of regularity.

10. Wright, *The Poet in the Poem* (Berkeley, 1962), pp. 31–32. For additional discussion of the poet as "singer," see F. C. Prescott, *Poetry and Myth* (New York, 1927), p. 40, and Susanne K. Langer, *Feeling and Form* (New York, 1953), pp. 249ff.

Of *Balme*, of *Oyle*, of *Spice*, and *Amber-Greece*.
I sing of *Times trans-shifting*; and I write
How *Roses* first came *Red*, and *Lillies White*.
I write of *Groves*, of *Twilights*, and I sing
The Court of *Mab*, and of the *Fairie-King*.
I write of *Hell*; I sing (and ever shall)
Of *Heaven*, and hope to have it after all.[11]

The most obvious feature of the persona in this poem is his epic concern to sing of all creation. He begins with simple, and literal, natural objects. The second line presents yet another object, identical in substance to those in line 1, but qualified by temporal adjectives. This addition emphasizes the seasonal order of the realm in which the

---

11. L. C. Martin, in his edition of *The Poetical Works of Robert Herrick* (Oxford, 1956), calls attention to the similarity between this poem and Thomas Bastard's *de subiecto operis sui*, but cites only four lines. The poem is worth quoting in its entirety:

> I speake of wants, of frauds, of policies,
> Of manners, and of vertues and of times,
> Of vnthrifts and of friends, and enemies,
> Poets, Physitions, Lawyers, and Diuines,
> Of vsurers, buyers, borowers, ritch and poore,
> Of theeues, and murtherers, by sea and land,
> Of pickthankes, lyers, flatterers, lesse and more,
> Of good and bad, and all that comes to hand;
> I speake of hidden and of open things:
> Of strange euents, of countries farre and wide,
> Of warres, of captaynes, Nobles, Princes, kings,
> *Asia, Europe,* and all the world beside
>   This is my subiect, reader, I confesse,
>   From which I thinke seldome I doe disgresse.

(*Chrestoleros* [1598], I,i; *The Spenser Society Reprints*, 47 [1888], 1–2)
The most interesting feature of the comparison is a complete difference in tone: Herrick is serious and celebratory; Bastard is comic and satiric. Further, although both poets attempt to be comprehensive, the attempt yields distinct effects: Herrick's attempt results in a sense of order, integration, and completeness; Bastard's, a sense of accumulating chaos, destruction, and disharmony. Nevertheless there are striking similarities. For instance, at line 9, Bastard's poem alters its focus to speak of "hidden and of open things," of "strange euents," and of "all the world." This progression from the specific in the octave to causal factors and a more comprehensive overview in the sestet is precisely the same structural shift in focus that Herrick makes in his sonnet. Finally, the refocusing of attention in the concluding couplet, not on the subject of the verse, but on the speaker of that verse, is identical in both poems.

natural objects are found and implies an extra-literal dimension to the flowers. Presumably, April flowers are in some way quite different from July flowers, despite their material similarity. With the third line the singer enlarges his field to include human objects, and in the fourth line introduces the humans themselves. The temporal, seasonal order of line 2 is extended to include the human realm of this couplet and the extra-literal implications are expanded to a symbolic level as the subjects of both lines are explicitly ritualistic.

In the fifth line the speaker uses the word "write" for the first time, a word which has disturbed several critics.[12] He "writes" of youth and love, two states of human existence, or more probably given the careful progression of the poem, two symbolic activities; and because he "writes" of them, he is able to "sing" of "cleanly-*Wantonnesse*." The "writing" of line 5 (as well as lines 9, 11, and 13) is simply a further explanation of the activity about which the speaker is concerned: writing and singing, to the poet, are the same act—the act of poetic creation.

In the seventh line the speaker refers to the "spices" of the natural realm, maintaining his tendency to present the natural object first, its human equivalent second. Consequently, in the next line, he lists the human or man-made counterparts of the "*Dewes*" and "*Raines.*" The couplet continues the poem's elevation of the literal objects of both nature and man by suggesting their symbolic potentials. In the ninth line the speaker picks up the hints concerning time in lines 2, 3, and 5, and relates this transience to the underlying cause of things through the synecdochic and symbolic use of "*Roses*" and "*Lillies.*" In the final quatrain he moves beyond the natural and human realms to supernatural ones: first to "*Groves*" and "*Twilights*," in one sense totally natural, but because of position in the sonnet and connotation obviously more figurative; then to the quasi-human and pagan, yet still supernatural, fairy realms; and finally to Hell and Heaven, the ultimate supernatural realms.[13]

12. See, for example, Edward L. Hirsh, "Herrick's 'The Argument of his Book,' " *Explicator* 2 (1943): 11.
13. Cf. Patrick's note on the progression of the poem and Sidney Musgrove's

By the final line of the poem any distinction between "write" and "sing" is obliterated. By using both words, however, Herrick is able to associate the role of the singer with the craft of the poet: the singer-persona is the poet-persona. The identification might prove more significant than it first appears: in having his "singer" present a microcosmic view of his total reality (note that the final supernatural realms are just as real to this persona as brooks and blossoms), Herrick implies that the volume which this poem indexes is a world complete in itself, albeit an artistically contrived world. Within that world, as within the poem, specific points of emphasis can be isolated. A desire for comprehensiveness is certainly one. An understanding of the unity underlying creation is a second, most evident in the subtle relationships the persona draws between one object and another. This emphasis can perhaps be expanded by noting that the combination of all the various elements into a single poetic statement, into one "song," implies that all are of equal interest to the poet. The persona's concern with time in both the natural and the human realms is a third point of emphasis; in fact, time is one aspect which unites these two realms. Finally, and most important, is the persona's concern with singing: though he "sings" of various objects, the major emphasis is placed on the act of singing itself rather than the objects sung, and therefore on the completed song. By thus calling attention to the singer-persona, and to itself as a conscious song, the sonnet establishes an attitude toward the poetic act which unites all the poems in the remainder of the volume.

It has been suggested that the shift in point of view in the final line destroys the integrity of "The Argument." The persona of the first thirteen lines shows no relation to his material other than celebration; in the final line this attitude gives way to one of "hope,"[14] an emotional state incongruent to the nature of the established speaker. In fact, the shift in point of view is a shift in persona.[15] The poet goes out of his way to tell the reader he has been listening to a poetic speaker;

discussion in "The Universe of Robert Herrick," *Auckland University College Bulletin* 38, English Series 4 (1950): 5–6.

14. Cf. H. R. Swardson, *Poetry and the Fountain of Light* (Columbia, Mo., 1962), who sees a tone of self-defensiveness and defiance in these lines (p. 47).

15. Wright, *The Poet in the Poem*, pp. 38–39.

he jolts the reader out of the comfortable and secure experience of public celebration into a world of private human desire and (possible) frustration. Rather than destroying the poem's integrity, however, the change in persona may be functional as the intrusion of the "hopeful" voice clarifies and emphasizes the existence of the "singing" one. Furthermore, the shift signals a basic rhetorical pattern for the volume as a whole by implying that the peculiar sensibilities of Herrick the private man will be objectified and presented through the guise of a formal and public celebrator.

Assuming, then, that the "Argument" presents the main "singing" persona of the *Hesperides* as a whole, it is possible to define him with more precision. Because he is a singer, he is also a celebrator, and celebration is, in the final analysis, a mode of viewing reality. That is, we can question reality, in which case we use a dialectical mode; we can ridicule reality by means of an ironic mode; we can castigate reality, in which case we use a satiric mode; we can assert reality by means of a naturalistic mode; we can extend reality through an allegorical mode; or we can celebrate reality with the ceremonial mode. This classification, of course, does not claim to be either comprehensive or fixed; as recent criticism testifies, "modes" have a habit of expanding and contracting at frequently alarming rates. Nevertheless, if we can accept at all the conception of a "mode of poetic expression," then the serviceability of that conception depends upon how accurately one mode can be distinguished from all the others, even if those distinctions are purely hypothetical.

The "I sing" of "The Argument" is therefore much more than a statement of poetic intent: it is an assertion of poetic achievement. For when a poet "sings" of anything (an act, an object, a person), that thing must be integrated within his completed view of reality. In a dialectical mode, for instance, the poet generally experiments with and questions various aspects of his reality. John Donne, for example, uses a dialectical persona to present images and ideas which at first seem to have no logical relation to other images and ideas in his particular vision. He then has the persona attempt, though he may fail, to integrate those images and ideas into a view of experience which the poet (or the priest) can accept. The dialectical mode is consequently a seeking after correspondences and relies upon a rhetoric of skepticism and experimentation. In the ceremonial mode, however, the decision to celebrate of necessity implies that the integration has already taken place. The reader may be aware at times of some struggle in the persona's mind to fit things into a coherent pattern, but that struggle could never take the form of overt questioning, as that would qualify the celebration. The persona of a Herrick poem takes the reader beyond the seeking of correspondences to a public rejoicing over them. The ceremonial is therefore an optimistic mode whose rhetoric is dogmatic and whose generic forms are usually conventional rather than experimental.[16]

The "poetic ceremonial," then, is a mode of viewing reality which celebrates integrated and completed experiences.[17] Though abstract itself, such a conception of ceremonial poetry suggests general limits on four poetic elements: the subject, the form, the tone, and the intended reader-response. The first of these, the subject, is obviously awkward to discuss precisely before examining individual poems. Theoretically, there are no inherent restrictions against any specific subjects and all matters can be treated ceremonially. However, the mode does imply restriction on the *kinds* of subjects treated. If, as suggested above, the ceremonial always or even usually presents integrated and completed experiences, it will not normally argue a thesis or tentatively explore an issue. This is not to say that ceremonial poems never contain theses or do not treat real issues, simply that their focus is not on the argument itself: whatever the poem "argues" is, in a real sense, a by-product of the *action* which it praises. In "The Argument," for example, we could isolate two principal themes: the unity of

16. On the distinction between "rhetoric of experiment" and "rhetoric of convention," see Hiram Haydn, *The Counter-Renaissance* (New York, 1950), pp. 15–17. For Haydn, a poet's commitment to one rhetorical form or the other is determined by whether he is, generally speaking, a romantic (experimental) or a classicist (conventional). With admitted simplification, "dialectical" and "ceremonial" could be substituted for the latter pair of terms.

17. Cf. Mircea Eliade, *Cosmos and History: The Myth of the Eternal Return*, trans. Willard R. Trask (New York, 1954), who sees the "end" of ceremony as "the restoration of integral wholeness" (p. 25).

existence and the hierarchical interrelationships between individual objects. But neither thesis is *argued*, though each is presented; rather, Herrick demonstrates both by "singing" (i.e., praising) all elements of his reality equally. By this means, the *act* of celebration becomes the real subject of the poem and the two ostensible theses become either subordinated or simply assumed. In the same way, when Herrick writes an epitaph, he subordinates death, or the destructive force of time, which might be taken as the dialectical thesis, to the celebratory response to or action taken as a result of that death. It would be possible, therefore, to call this ceremonial poetry mimetic rather than didactic except that the critical difficulties involved in such an opposition obscure the point. For the moment it will suffice to emphasize that "ceremonial" refers to the *action* of a poem, not to any argument that action might support; and that poems written in this mode do not literally explore or confute an issue, but *demonstrate* an action whose worth is already assumed.[18] Finally, in terms of the subject, "ceremonial" implies that the actions depicted in the poem may in fact be literal ceremonies or rituals—actions, that is, in which the progressive steps are clearly drawn and in which the formal bounds are well defined. And, like all rituals, the poetic ceremonial may be, in some way, a means of celebrating, through public and formal expression, a communal belief or faith.

The form of a ceremonial poem is the most difficult and the most critical element to define—the most critical because the very conception of a ceremonial *mode* is a formal one; the most difficult because

18. This distinction is equivalent to that drawn in classical rhetoric between judicial and deliberative oratory on the one hand and demonstrative oratory on the other. The first two, concerned with *arguing* what is just or expedient, must make full use of Proof and Refutation (two of the standard six or seven parts of a typical oration). The latter, concerned with praising or blaming rather than contending, does not *prove* at all: it can omit both sections of the oration because it merely amplifies (i.e., demonstrates) propositions set forth as certain from the beginning. See Cicero, *De partitione oratoria*, ed. & trans. H. Rackham, Loeb Classical Library (London, 1942), p. 365. See also D. J. Gordon's discussion of the Goddess Ceremony in "Chapman's 'Hero and Leander'," *English Miscellany* 5 (1954): 57ff.; C. S. Lewis's discussion of the same figure in "Hero and Leander," *Proceedings of the British Academy* 38 (1952): 30 and *passim*; and my own "Epideictic Rhetoric and the Renaissance Lyric," *Journal of Medieval and Renaissance Studies* 3 (1973): 203–31.

form itself is so slippery a critical term. Without trying to be arbitrarily prescriptive, "form," as I have used it, means what R. S. Crane calls the "shaping or directing cause" which gives to the work of art a "quality of organic wholeness" (i.e., a perceivable this-ness, quiddity), and which involves "the particular conceptual form [the] subject is to take . . . , the particular mode of argument or of rhetoric [used] in discussing it, and the particular end [the] discussion is to serve."[19] That is, form is *not* synonymous with structure—not rhyme pattern, stanzaic pattern, or even narrative-thematic pattern; it is itself an abstract *formative* idea by which the poet selects and orders those elements of his experience appropriate to the specific poem.[20] To repeat an earlier definition in formal terms, the poetic ceremonial isolates specific and limited instants of human experience and transforms them into static rituals (the conceptual form the subject is to take), celebrates through praise the significance of those rites (the mode of rhetoric used), and attempts to get the reader himself to participate in the rite (the particular end of the poem).

Formally, the most obvious feature of the ceremonial mode is its desire to transform all the activities it treats into rituals. Those actions which are literal rites (e.g., Herrick's Hock-cart) it magnifies; those which are not it ritualizes. It would seem, of course, that much of Herrick's verse which deals with literal rites (the fairy poems, the Candlemasse poems, the charms, the poems on household deities, and so forth) *minimizes* rather than *magnifies* ritual. But even in those poems where the poet's observing eye diminishes the objects to minia-

---

19. *The Languages of Criticism and the Structure of Poetry* (Toronto, 1953), pp. 141–42. Crane unfortunately complicates matters by using "form" within his definition and his use of "mode" is not quite the same as my own. Still, his understanding of the scope of form in its largest sense is invaluable.

20. My conception of "form" also owes a considerable debt to Francis Fergusson's brilliant discussions of Aristotelian "action" in "*Macbeth* as the Imitation of an Action," *English Institute Essays, 1951* (New York, 1952) and *The Idea of a Theater* (Princeton, 1949). On the ceremonial's relation to form, see Deming, "The Classical Ceremonial": "He [Herrick] uses ceremonial as a formal, organizing principle whereby the entire poem is the ceremony, or where ceremonial forms part of the orderly poetic structure" (p. 23); and Gordon's discussion of how both Jonson and Chapman view ceremony as "form" in an Aristotelian sense ("Chapman's 'Hero and Leander'," pp. 67–68).

ture status (e.g., "The Fairie Temple"), the ritualizing process itself always dilates to larger symbolic forms. In a sense, it could be argued that each poem participates in two concurrent motions. The first transforms the literal event on which Herrick has focused into a significant ritual. By holding the event up to microscopic and detailed view, Herrick demonstrates that it consists of a carefully controlled sequence, a precise order of parts, and a completed unit of action. In turn, this demonstration frequently yields a three-part narrative structure to the poems: an exhortation to participate in the ceremony, a depiction of the ceremony itself, and an implicit or explicit statement on the significance of the ceremony. Even when his scheme is not so clear, the intent is the same: to give private actions more meaning than they would have in literal, experiential terms by turning the smallest of details into important parts of a public rite. The second motion of the poems carries the process a step further: particular rites continuously dilate to the broader communal duties of commemoration and worship. The implications of this process can be seen in Herrick's treatment of both Christian and pagan rites. As he strips those rites down to their essential celebratory forms, the forms themselves begin to accrue more and more symbolic meanings. We end the poems by responding only in part to the specific rite invoked; an equal part of our response is directed toward a ritualistic approach to life itself on all its levels. The process of diminishing becomes, paradoxically, the highest amplification as the elemental form of all the rites reminds us that all are connected, that all play an essential part in the sacrament of life itself.

The tone of a ceremonial poem is, relatively speaking, more constant than those in other modes. For instance, a speaker can be satiric, ironic, or inquisitive with varying degrees of intensity or fervor, but a celebratory singer is by definition committed to praise which is intense and unqualified. He is both optimistic and festive in response to experience and dogmatic in affirming the value of the ritualistic action he presents. In the same way that the speaker of an epigram presumes a universal agreement with his point, so the affirmative tone of the ceremonial poet presupposes a public, communal rejoicing over the subject praised. Naturally, the assumption that the affirmative tone of ceremonial is fairly "constant" does not preclude an infinite variety of pitches within and among poems, nor does it limit the ceremonial poet to the solemn seriousness of a priest; it simply means that the poet's relationship to his subject is rarely in doubt as it might be in the dialectical mode. As stated earlier, the dialectical poet often questions the very value of his subject; for the ceremonial poet, that value is never an issue.

In part, the audience response to a ceremonial poem has already been defined: acceptance of and rejoicing over the integrated view of experience which the poem presents. But this is only part of the response. By either presenting or constructing a literal ritual the poet tries to actualize in the reader a festive response similar to his own. He tries to engage him, in other words, in an actual participation in the rite which the poem depicts. If he does his task well, the presentation of the Hock-cart, for example, will allow the reader to experience the harvest-home festival as he experiences the poem. In turn, the reader will join his voice with the poet's in celebrating the ultimate significance of this rite.

To return to an earlier definition, the ceremonial mode performs two major functions: it provides ritual form to otherwise non-ritual actions (or further heightens the symbolic form of pre-existing rites) and it celebrates the value of ritual in human experience. As a specifically *poetic* mode, however, it accomplishes one more feat. By elevating and formalizing literal actions it freezes those actions in a realm peculiar to art itself. In "The Argument," the "singing" of "*Brooks*, of *Blossomes, Birds*, and *Bowers*" is not only an assertion of the value of these objects, but an attempt to free them from the transitory condition of the natural realm and to transport them into the eternal stasis of "song."[21] There is, of course, a great danger of oversimplification at this point, for all poems, as works of art, exist in a special "timeless" realm; the mere presence of artistic stasis, therefore, cannot be used to characterize this particular mode. Still, there do seem to be some distinguishing features in the ceremonial

21. Wright, *The Poet in the Poem*, p. 31.

poet's attitude toward and his use of the stasis his art effects. Some of those features may be suggested by differentiating between "closed" and "open" poems.

In attributing significance to their subject matters, most modes of poetic expression refer to elements outside the poem—other experiences, other ideas, other actions. These modes seek always to extend beyond the poetry itself. What is required of the reader, or expected of him, also transcends the actual poem. He must make an additional step of amalgamating what the poem presents with his own situation, either emotionally, intellectually, or actively. In a satiric poem, for instance, the "mirror" functions only as a starting point, for the exposure of human foibles is not an end in itself: it expects and demands further effort on the part of the reader to rectify his own life-style. This action is clearly beyond the limits of the literal poem. Similarly, one of the major functions of the dialectical mode would seem to be to jolt the reader out of his comfortable preconceptions and to force him to re-examine himself and his surroundings. Consequently, the sonnets of Shakespeare and Donne, however dissimilar, are alike in raising more questions than they answer. The reader cannot end many of these poems "satisfied"; he knows that more is expected of him on the basis of what the poem has presented. Both the satiric and the dialectic poems are "open": they consciously and deliberately lead out from the poem itself to actions which are not poetic; they *use* poetry as a means of moving the reader from security to insecurity.[22]

In the ceremonial mode such is not the case. The reader is not referred to elements outside the poem and is not expected to commit further action on the basis of what is given in the poem. Of course, no reader comes to a poem devoid of other experiences, and no poem of any value can fail to affect the reader's "extra-poetic" life. The point is rather that the consciousness of the ceremonial poem is directed inwards, not outwards: the reader is not asked to *do* anything more than experience the poem. That experience itself is made as deliber-

22. The best treatment of the "openness" of the dialectical mode and its effects on the reader is Stanley Fish's *Self-Consuming Artifacts* (Berkeley, 1972).

ately satisfying and complete as possible. In this sense, the ceremonial poem is a "closed" form: the poetic experience does not point itself toward any other kind of action.[23]

As mentioned above, all poems, as poems, share the static nature of a completed artistic whole, regardless of the mode of expression used. Stasis in this sense can be defined as temporal fixity, stability, and permanence. Any art work is temporally bounded by the form in which it is cast; within the limits of that form, time may progress, but as a completed whole the work has been removed from temporal control altogether. We acknowledge this fact, of course, by using the present tense to refer to the actions of a given character; we recognize that each time the poem or novel is read the character re-acts whatever he is doing. Time is "fixed" in an eternal present. As Susanne Langer puts it, "the lyric poet creates a sense of concrete reality from which the time element has been canceled out, leaving a Platonic sense of 'eternity.' "[24]

While it is surely an oversimplification to claim that the stasis created by most modes of poetry is merely a by-product of the poetic process, it can be argued that the stasis is not acknowledged by the poems themselves. What has been said above concerning the directing of the reader to actions and thoughts external to the poem and subsequent to his experience of the poem demonstrates that the created stasis is not fundamental to the poet's intent. In the ceremonial mode, however, the artistic stasis is of fundamental importance because it provides the ultimate significance to the ritual itself. That is, the literal actions which the poet treats become meaningful as they take on ritualistic patterns;

23. Cf. Whitaker's argument that Herrick's poems do refer outside themselves ("Herrick and the Fruits of the Garden," p. 16). He is answering a statement made by F. R. Leavis in *Revaluation* (New York, 1963; orig. pub. 1947): "Herrick's game, Herrick's indulgence, in fact, is comparatively solemn; it does not refer us outside itself. 'Let us,' he virtually says, 'be sweetly and deliciously sad,' and we are to be absorbed in the game, the 'solemn' rite" (p. 40). Certainly Whitaker is right in arguing that what we learn from a Herrick poem has application beyond that poem; but he is not right in claiming Leavis misunderstands Herrick, for while the latter is not talking explicitly about the poet's mode of expression, he does see the "bounded" and "closed" nature of the ceremonial to which Herrick invites us.

24. *Feeling and Form*, p. 268.

in turn, the clearest instance of the meaning ritual provides is its ability to free the act from the general transitory state of existence and to freeze it in a permanent form. The act gains final status by being "fixed" as an autonomous thing rather than being seen as simply a process. Both poet and reader, in their experience with the poem, are able to share in this sense of permanence, first by not being called upon to commit further actions *after* they have completed the poem and second by participating fully in the rite. The second point is explained by Mircea Eliade: "the abolition of profane time [i.e., temporal sequence] and the individual's projection into mythic time [i.e., eternal "time"] do not occur, of course, except at essential periods—those, that is, when the individual is truly himself: *on the occasion of rituals* or of important acts [my italics]."[25]

As it applies to the *Hesperides*, however, we cannot fully understand the nature of this poetic mode without making some attempt to discover the causal factors committing the poet to it rather than to some other mode. Perhaps such causes could be located by claiming that Herrick's special sensibility feels the need to accentuate certain activities as a means of making us more human or better humans. Certainly there is a sense in which this feeling must have been present. Or perhaps it could be claimed that in the rapidly altering and, in some ways, deteriorating world of the seventeenth century the poet tries to grasp those things to which he can cling with some surety. These little ceremonies actually become a means of escaping the unsure real world into the more stable world of the imagination.[26] There is a sense in which this motive seems to have been operative also. But neither answer is finally satisfactory, for only when we emphasize how often this poet of delicate sentiment, this creator of what have been called delightful miniatures, shows his concern with the problems of mutability and the utter reality of death, do we approach a viable understanding of the importance of this particular mode to him.

In most of his poetry, though to varying extents, Herrick attempts

25. *Cosmos and History*, p. 35. See also Malcolm M. Ross's discussion of time and ritual in *Poetry and Dogma* (New Brunswick, 1954), pp. 38ff.
26. Whitaker, "Herrick and the Fruits of the Garden," pp. 21 and *passim*.

to go beyond what is transient, mutable, dying.[27] This is not to say that it is escapist poetry, for the poet and his personae are far from denying the realities of change and death. But Herrick's need seems to have been to create a realm of stasis, of immutability and transcendence, which would render death as more significant than simply the end of the natural process (a process he defines as leading only to "Putrefaction"), or which would render the life preceding this death as more significant than simply a path to the one inevitable end. That realm is continually sought by means of the poetic ceremonial. The transformation of dying and death into significant ceremonial activities heightens and intensifies the meaning of the ceremony itself and allows the poet (and the reader), if only for the duration of the poem, to transcend the fact of death. And the celebration of specific ceremonial activities in human experience creates a stasis upon which death (again for the duration of the poem) does not impinge. What these ceremonial activities are, how the stasis is created, and how the formal nature of the poem affects both will be analyzed in the following chapters devoted to the kinds of "songs" sung by Herrick's four main singer-personae.

27. The idea that death and transience are significant themes in the *Hesperides* is not, of course, a new one, but it has not been emphasized nearly enough. Among those studies which have treated the motifs, see Allan H. Gilbert, "Robert Herrick on Death," *Modern Language Quarterly* 5 (1944): 61–67; Whitaker's "Herrick and the Fruits of the Garden"; and two articles by Robert Deming, "Robert Herrick's Classical Ceremonial," and "Herrick's Funeral Poems," *Studies in English Literature* 9 (1969): 153–67. Of the book-length studies, only Rollin (*Robert Herrick*) comes close to recognizing the seriousness with which Herrick confronts these issues.

CHAPTER II

THE PASTORAL
CEREMONIAL

THE CONCERNS of Herrick's first major persona, the pastoral singer, are varied: he celebrates man's intimate and harmonious relationship with nature; he stresses the peace and contentment of the rural dweller; he sings the necessity of seizing the country joys while they last; and he occasionally tries to escape his sometimes harsh and oppressive surroundings by withdrawing to a more Arcadian setting. These conventional motifs, derived mainly from Horace's *"beatus ille"* Epode and Virgil's praise of *agricola* in *Georgics* II, focus on the question of human happiness, or the qualities of the happy man.[1]

The first of these concerns is seen most clearly in the persona's reliance on analogy and metaphor to draw micro-macrocosmic correspondences. In "Corinna's going a Maying," for example, the subtle shifts of emphasis from the mistress as now a literal part of the natural realm, then distinct from it, but always a participator in it, suggest one of the metaphoric ways Herrick delineates and celebrates the man-nature relationship. In fact, these metaphoric correspondences are drawn so often and so freely by the pastoral persona that the reader tends to lose track of them as "correspondences." He begins, that is, to think of Corinna as an element of nature, and of roses and meadows as having human qualities and functions.

The second concern or motif of the pastoral persona is the contentment of the rural man. Whether he praises internal or external content, the speaker's attitude is essentially Stoic in equating serenity, self-possession, and peace (*otium*) with the good, or happy, life (*vita*

---

1. The fullest treatment of Herrick's pastoralism is Roger Rollin's *Robert Herrick*. For general studies of the specific motifs given here see Maren-Sofie Røstvig, *The Happy Man: Studies in the Metamorphoses of a Classical Ideal* 2nd edition (Oslo, 1962), I, 41ff., and Miner's chapter on "The Good Life" in *The Cavalier Mode*, pp. 43–99.

bona or *vita beata*). This Stoic ethic, which appears in such poems as "A Country life," usually emphasizes moderation, the acceptance of all things in measure. In its ethical sense, moderation is analogous to the medieval doctrine of *mesure* as applied to country needs and desires. The country life is the contented life because it offers only what is necessary, and thereby curbs the greed and ambition to which urban men inevitably fall prey. Such an ethos is the basis for the frequent opposition in these poems between country and courtly, pastoral and urban. Seneca provides a convenient summary of this Stoic concern in the *Dialogues*:

> And with this measure we shall be content if we have learned to be content. . . . We must habituate ourselves to reject ostentation and value things by their utility, not by their trappings. . . . We must learn to strengthen self-restraint, curb luxury, temper, ambition, moderate anger, view poverty calmly, cultivate frugality. . . .[2]

The third concern of the pastoral persona is seen in his various treatments of the *carpe diem* motif. He seeks always to "seize the day," not in the wanton spirit often associated with the Horatian phrase, but in a true Epicurean grasping of the present for its own sake and for the joys which it brings. Like the Epicureans, this persona proposes a serious pleasure-pain ethic of squeezing the best that remains out of life. As Norman DeWitt has stated, "the brevity and uncertainty of life were naturally a commonplace of Greek thought. The originality of Epicurus consisted in lifting this commonplace from the rank of a sentiment to that of a motive of action."[3] The *carpe diem* injunction,

---

2. "On Tranquility," quoted in *The Stoic Philosophy of Seneca: Essays and Letters*, ed. & trans. Moses Hadas (New York, 1968), p. 91. See also Seneca's "Moderation," No. 5, *Letters to Lucilius*. Roger Rollin views this Stoic moderation as the synthesizing ethos of the entire *Hesperides* (*Robert Herrick*, pp. 74, 84–85, 91). This emphasis on the *ethical* meaning of moderation needs, however, to be balanced by Paul R. Jenkins' reminder that Herrick is rarely as Stoical as Horace or even as Ben Jonson, and that he often translates ethical maxims into aesthetic terms, at times into questions of appetite, which are hardly "moderate." See "Rethinking What Moderation Means to Robert Herrick," *English Literary History* 39 (1972): 49–65.

3. Norman Wentworth DeWitt, *Epicurus and his Philosophy* (New York, 1967), p. 183.

therefore, is not simply a call to seduction, but a philosophical motive for all human endeavors.

The final concern of the pastoral persona is the presentation of an idyllic, Arcadian existence, one which takes him beyond the bounds of the mutable to a realm of serenity and bliss. Herrick's poetry offers several variations of this concern: the pastoral dream of the Elysian Fields in "The Apparition of his Mistresse calling him to Elizium"; the withdrawal to a joyous and harmonious existence in "A Country life"; even the pastoral visions of a quiet grave decked with flowers and surrounded by mourning flower-maidens. All of these are versions of the idyllic; all are, to some extent, an escape from the literal confrontation of death and mutability.[4]

Though these four concerns are the principal motifs of Herrick's pastoral vision, his pastoral persona can be defined more precisely by noting that he appears in not one, but at least three, guises. All three are clearly pastoral, but quite distinct in terms of the subject matters which they treat and the types of statements they are likely to make in any given poem. At the risk of overschematizing, these guises can be termed the classical, the domestic, and the artistic.

The classical-pastoral persona is the conventional "bucolic" singer:

4. It is instructive to compare these four motifs with those seen by Røstvig (*The Happy Man*, I, 41–45) as common to the "beatus ille" convention. There are five major themes, she says, in this tradition, which may appear separately or in conjunction with one or more of the others: (1) Happiness is a question of *internal* peace; the Happy Man, he who is self-possessed and serene. (2) The obscure life of the husbandman provides the Happy Man with *external* peace. In Herrick, these two themes are generally combined into one. (3) The Happy Man is he who gains a knowledge of the universe by studying the causes of things. One could argue that Herrick's concern with "correspondences" gives him "a knowledge of his universe" and is thus equivalent to this motif. But Røstvig has a specific passage of Virgil in mind here (ll. 475–512 of *Georgics* II), and to ally Herrick with the Virgilian philosopher-poet would be a distortion of each. This motif, in Herrick's verse, is simply on a less abstract philosophical plane. (4) The country life offers truer and more genuine pleasures than the courtly or urban life; and (5) the country life represents a veritable Golden Age or Earthly Paradise. Røstvig goes on to align these motifs with philosophical traditions: "Motifs 1 and 2 are Stoic in character, and the poetry in which they are found is austere in mood. The third is intellectual in its austerity, while the fourth and fifth admit Epicurean ideas. . . ." The whole tradition, then, hovers between Stoicism and Epicureanism, though these terms must be taken as attitudes toward experience rather than intellectual disciplines.

he exploits the opposition between city and country in order to emphasize the blessings of a simple life close to nature. By calling the persona "classical" I do not mean to imply Herrick's indebtedness to specific writers, though the general influence of Virgil, Horace, Tibullus, and Propertius, among others, is perfectly clear.[5] The universality of the themes this persona presents often precludes asserting with any surety particular sources and, in fact, one of the main reasons for Herrick's use of the pastoral voice at all is the very traditional nature of the classical-pastoral ethos. That is, Herrick does not use the Latin poets because he wholeheartedly agrees with the view of reality which they present, or because he wishes he were "a Roman free born," or even because he is, as he sometimes claims, a "Roman" poet—he adopts the guise of the classical pastoralist because it represents a familiar and clearly defined approach to existence. He can therefore adapt it, play with it, mock it, alter it, qualify it—all without losing the essential nature of the tradition, or without losing the reader's understanding of that tradition.

In general, the classical-pastoral persona is the most philosophical of the three in the sense that he argues the value of the pastoral life in traditional, abstract terms. For this reason, his poems make constant use of the Stoic and Epicurean conventions given above. He is basically optimistic and affirmative regarding the things of this world, although implicit in his arguments is a recognition of the transience of the world.

The domestic-pastoral persona is similar to the classical, but there is one specific difference: the classical persona treats man's existence in general terms and presents his portrait of the good life in exemplary fashion, unlocalized and abstract; the domestic persona places these abstract formulae in local settings, provides a greater emphasis on real

5. The major source studies of Herrick's poetry are P. Nixon, "Herrick and Martial," *Classical Philology* 5 (1910) : 189–202; Delattre's *Robert Herrick*; Pauline Aiken, "Influence of the Latin Elegists"; McEuen, *Classical Influence upon the Tribe of Ben*; Melville J. Ruggles, "Horace and Herrick," *Classical Journal* 31 (1936) : 223–34; Graydon W. Regenos, "The Influence of Horace on Robert Herrick," *Philological Quarterly* 26 (1947) : 268–84; Deming, "The Classical Ceremonial"; and, of course, the editions of Martin and Patrick.

folk customs, and demonstrates in specific instances the working out of the classical ideals.[6] He is more concerned with fairy tales, charms, local legends, local ceremonies, even local gossip, and his poems always yield a sense of "felt" experience and place-setting. The philosophical basis of the pastoral is not neglected, but neither is it the focus of the speaker's vision. The domestic persona is less interested in the ethos of the pastoral than in the sheer joys of country living; he depicts those joys, not because they are analogous to a given philosophical system, but simply because they are joys—they demonstrate man's capacity to "enjoy" his time.

The artistic-pastoral persona is but one more step removed. He strips away any philosophical significance other than that attached to the act of celebrating. He still represents a pastoral voice because his subject matter is the simple elements of nature and man's country existence, but whatever ethical formulae he does posit hinge on aesthetic rather than pastoral ideals. He is concerned to show that the act of enjoyment itself, regardless of the thing being enjoyed, is of value. In this sense, he is still relatively close to the domestic persona. What distinguishes him from that guise is, first, his use of both unlocalized and localized incidents, of the abstract and the literal. Second, even more than the domestic persona, he attempts to turn all experiences into ritualistic acts and to give those acts meaning primarily because they are ritualistic. Whereas the domestic persona might see the significance of the bringing in of the grain in the joyous feelings of a job well done or in the festive simplicity of the rustics' merriment, the artistic persona sees the meaning of the "hock-cart" in the ritualistic celebration of a static moment in which workers and landlord are literally and symbolically united. This artistic guise, moreover, may be operative in poems spoken by either of the other pastoral voices, giving import and form to what they say.

Before turning to the poetry itself, a final word on these "guises" is

6. Cf. Delattre's assertion that the pastoral mode "se dépouille peu à peu de son attirail de vagues formules surannées pour se revêtir d'une grâce plus précise et plus vigoureuse, pour adopter une allure qui, par sa libre franchise enfin, sent déjà le plein air" (*Robert Herrick*, p. 280) ; and McEuen's reference to Herrick's "true English pastorals" (*Classical Influence*, pp. 193–94).

necessary because I have included some poems under the voice of the classical-pastoralist which would seem to be more appropriate to the domestic voice, and vice versa. Let me emphasize, therefore, that these categories are largely a matter of convenience to assist in defining what seem to be recognizable (i.e., distinct) personae. It would be fruitless, however, to insist that the boundaries of the categories are rigid or that some features of one speaking voice do not occasionally overlap those of another. The problem can easily be illustrated. "His content in the Country" (H-552) and "His Grange, or private wealth" (H-724) are treated here as classical-pastoral poems despite their biographical references to Prew, to sundry unusual pets, and to other specific details. In terms of the definitions given above, both poems would seem to fall under the domestic speaker's concentration on local setting and "felt" experience. In both poems, however, the precision of the details is misleading, and despite the localized portrait each seems to draw the primary concern of their persona is to make an ethical statement. His *use* of detail, in other words, is philosophical rather than dramatic and this feature defines him as a classical voice. Conversely, "Corinna's going a Maying" is here treated as a domestic-pastoral poem even though it presents a philosophical point and seems more generalized than localized. Here again the justification for placement rests on the speaker's dramatization: though a thesis is undeniably present in the poem, the "felt" experience which it depicts has assumed priority. In either case, though, the point is that the categories and the personae are not as rigid as my use of them implies; the guidelines suggested are practical rather than absolute.

i. THE CLASSICAL VOICE

Herrick introduces his pastoral voice in the second poem of the *Hesperides*, "To his Muse":

> WHither *Mad maiden* wilt thou roame?
> Farre safer 'twere to stay at home:
> Where thou mayst sit, and piping please
> The poore and private *Cottages*.

Since *Coats*, and *Hamlets*, best agree
With this thy meaner Minstralsie.
There with the Reed, thou mayst expresse
The Shepherds Fleecie happinesse:
And with thy *Eclogues* intermixe
Some smooth, and harmless *Beucolicks*.
There on a Hillock thou mayst sing
Unto a handsome Shephardling;
Or to a Girle (that keeps the Neat)
With breath more sweet then Violet.
There, there, (perhaps) such Lines as These
May take the simple *Villages*.
But for the Court, the Country wit
Is despicable unto it.
Stay then at home, and doe not goe
Or flie abroad to seeke for woe.
Contempts in Courts and Cities dwell;
No *Critick* haunts the Poore mans Cell:
Where thou mayst hear thine own Lines read
By no one tongue, there, censured.
That man's unwise will search for Ill,
And may prevent it, sitting still.

Literally, the poem can be classified as a planctus and functions, in conjunction with the succeeding ones (H-3 through H-7), as a parody on the "Go, litel bok" motif. The persona complains that the censorious court will not appreciate the simple songs of a pastoral singer and that any attempt to gain the court's favor with such frivolities is doomed to failure, or scorn. The persona is a familiar shepherd-singer, a Colin Clout figure, which Herrick often uses in such complaint-lyrics.[7] He sings in the "humble style" ("meaner Minstralsie") as opposed to the (implied) more tortuous and conceited style of the court;

7. Compare "An Eclogue, or Pastorall between Endimion Porter and Lycidas Herrick" (H-492), and "A Dialogue betwixt himselfe and Mistresse Elizabeth Wheeler, under the name of Amarillis" (H-1068), both of which are formally and thematically related to "To his Muse."

his subjects are the joys of simple living ("the Shepherds Fleecie happinesse"); and his proper audience is the "simple *Villages*." The persona is, in other words, a classical-pastoralist: his subject is unlocalized, he presents no specific or real action, and he treats the contentment of the pastoral life in only the most general terms.

In the final section of the poem (ll. 16–26), the opposition implicit in the first part turns into blatant antagonism as the city, or courtly, audience becomes the active foe of the pastoral muse, is contemptuous of her and ridicules her. Such statements are familiar from other "pastoral" poets, but Herrick seems to go out of his way not merely to acknowledge but to establish the court's contempt for such verse. Line 18, for instance, with its enjambed rhythm, emphasizes the violence of the audience's feelings. The tone of the final ten lines jars with the portrait of the ostensibly simple and naïve persona of the first sixteen— it is more biting, more satiric than the reader expects of him. This incongruity between the speaker's established character and his adopted tone is a device Herrick frequently uses to direct the reader's attention to more subtle distinctions or qualifications. Here the incongruity reveals that beneath the surface humor the poem's function is polemical. The persona is more than a naïve pastoral singer: he is a self-conscious artist concerned to demonstrate to his audience the value of his work. The poem is a rhetorical ploy, a challenge in a way to the court, demanding its readers be more receptive (even if defensively so) to the pastoral muse by protesting the relevance of her verse. At this point in the volume, the persona does not define that relevance or attempt to convert his readers to any pastoral view of existence. Here message is far less important than rhetorical stance.

As stated earlier, the philosophical base upon which the classical-pastoral construct is built has two cornerstones, Stoicism and Epicureanism. Both doctrines are present in "His content in the Country" (H-552):

> HEre, here I live with what my Board,
> Can with the smallest cost afford.
> Though ne'r so mean the Viands be,
> They well content my *Prew* and me.

Or Pea, or Bean, or Wort, or Beet,
What ever comes, content makes sweet:
Here we rejoyce, because no Rent
We pay for our poore Tenement:
Wherein we rest, and never feare
The Landlord, or the Usurer.
The Quarter-day do's ne'r affright
Our Peacefull slumbers in the night.
We eate our own, and batten more,
Because we feed on no mans score:
But pitie those, whose flanks grow great,
Swel'd with the Lard of others meat.
We blesse our Fortunes, when we see
Our own beloved privacie:
And like our living, where w'are known
To very few, or else to none.

Thematically, the key word of the lyric is "content," and, as the fourth and sixth lines indicate, the word is taken in at least two senses. In the first instance, "content" is equivalent to satisfaction or happiness: it is a state of calm acceptance, an essentially passive situation in which the speaker and his Prew find themselves. This meaning is equivalent to the Stoic doctrine of austere indifference.[8] The second sense implies a more active role on the part of the speaker: instead of a passive condition, "content" is an attitude or means of approaching a given situation. Thus, "content makes sweet" suggests that the attitude of affirmative acceptance makes the situation easier, or better, or somehow more satisfying. Here the connotation is close to an Epicurean *carpe diem* thesis,[9] although the same sentiment occurs at times in Stoic

8. See Hadas, *The Stoic Philosophy of Seneca*, p. 24; Gilbert Highet, *The Classical Tradition* (New York, 1957), pp. 207–8; and Haydn, *The Counter-Renaissance*, p. 637.
9. The more "active" nature of the Epicurean ethos as opposed to the Stoic is suggested by the former's horror of procrastination. See Epicurus (Diogenes Laertius, *Lives of the Ancient Philosophers*, Loeb Classical Library [London, 1925], 122); Horace, *Epistles* I.ii.41–42; and Seneca, *Epistles* XIII.16 and XXIII.9.

thought as well. Content is, then, both an active approach to reality, embodying perhaps an entire ethos, and the resulting state this approach yields. The persona can be described in both senses: he is content with his lot and he is deliberate in making himself content with that lot.

The poem itself demonstrates contentment on both levels. The pastoral life contents the speaker because it presents him with just enough of everything. All his basic needs are fulfilled, which suggests a third meaning of "content," substance. Because the philosophical principle of moderation underlies this emphasis on contentment, the speaker is able to define the opposition between the pastoral and courtly lives by calling attention to urban aberrations from the moderate mean: the usurer lining his pocket with others' money, the glutton lining his stomach with others' food, the landlord continually presenting the threat of eviction, and the ever-present friends denying a man any privacy. By nature the country life excludes one from these oppressions and provides for a commitment to the principle of moderation.

The poem gives a philosophical basis for evaluating the pastoral vision, but it does not ask for a rational judgment on the validity of this basis simply because it fails to explore the concept of contentment beyond conventional and superficial oppositions. The reader is asked to respond, not with logical analysis, but with intuitive affirmation of the pastoral vision as the persona presents it.

Herrick also deals with the same theme of pastoral contentment in "His Grange, or private wealth" (H-724):

> THough Clock,
> To tell how night drawes hence, I've none,
> A Cock,
> I have, to sing how day drawes on.
> I have
> A maid (my *Prew*) by good luck sent,
> To save
> That little, Fates me gave or lent.
> A Hen
> I keep, which creeking day by day,

Tells when
She goes her long white egg to lay.
A goose
I have, which, with a jealous eare,
Lets loose
Her tongue, to tell what danger's neare.
A Lamb
I keep (tame) with my morsells fed,
Whose Dam
An Orphan left him (lately dead.)
A Cat
I keep, that playes about my House,
Grown fat,
With eating many a miching Mouse.
To these
A *Trasy* I do keep, whereby
I please
The more my rurall privacie:
Which are
But toyes, to give my heart some ease:
Where care
None is, slight things do lightly please.

Like "His content in the Country," the vision of the pastoral life is presented here in unlocalized and abstract terms, despite the seeming precision of the list. In both poems the speaker and his maid are simply character-pegs on which the idea of contentment is hung, and the details of the portrait are used mainly to support that thesis. The final four lines round off each poem by giving an inductive conclusion based on the preceding lists. Like "His content in the Country," "His Grange" celebrates a general view of existence and calls the reader to share that celebration.

There is a problem with the poem as a whole, however, a problem of tone and statement. The crux of the difficulty lies in the final four lines, ostensibly the aphoristic conclusion. The tone at this point is considerably different from that in "His content." A qualifying note is sounded in the use of "toyes," "some ease," "slight things," and "lightly please." [10] The whole phrase, "to give my heart some ease," strikes the same kind of note. Given the basis of the pastoral life as contentment, all of these are valid choices, but the words themselves, with their implications of insignificance, suggest either a pleading or a humorous self-mockery not present in the preceding poem. If the heart of the persona were actually content, there would be no need to "ease" it with protest or laughter. Tone here belies statement. Likewise, the relatively ambiguous use of "some" and "slight" serves only to underscore the pleading tone. There is a hint, then, that the pastoral vision of the poem is being qualified in some way. We do not know what does the qualifying, though the shift of perspective in the final lines might imply that the pastoral vision is being weighed against a broader truth. That truth is not clarified, however, and the persona's tone is hard to reconcile with the contentment for which he argues.

The seemingly provisional tone here raises further questions. At what point does such a tone or implication threaten the integrity of a poem's ceremonial form? Can the poet overtly suggest limitations to his celebratory act and still maintain the celebration? Is a humorous treatment of a subject antithetical to ceremonial praise? As Herrick persists in pitting his pastoral rites against the conception of transience they are supposed to negate, these questions become increasingly more important. Certainly in the present poem the discordant tones do threaten the effectiveness of the ceremonial. But such provisional implications do not always function in a disruptive manner, and the mere presence of qualifying notes need not destroy the poem's celebration. They can, in fact, amplify the meaning of the celebratory act by "placing" it in a larger context which admits both its significance *and* its limitations. That context, for Herrick's pastoral poems as well as his courtly ones, will be defined as the inevitability of human mortality. The significance of the poems' ceremonial stases is at times

10. Cf. John Kimmey, "Order and Form in Herrick's *Hesperides*," *Journal of English and Germanic Philology* 70 (1971): 264–65.

magnified by the poet's very insistence on the limits of those stases: the recognition of death emphasizes the need to celebrate life.

Three poems in which the classical persona explores more fully the philosophy behind his pastoral vision are "A Country life" (H-106), "The Country life" (H-662), and "A Paranaeticall, or Advisive Verse" (H-670). The first poem, addressed to Herrick's brother, Thomas, is perhaps the poet's best in this vein. It examines more exhaustively than either of the others the central motifs of the classical-pastoral view.[11]

The opening lines of "A Country life" present once more the opposition on which the classical vision is constructed—the essential antagonism between the city and the country. "THrice, and above, blest" is the brother for leaving the city in favor of the "Countries sweet simplicity." The religious overtones of the invocation tend to gloss over the hint in the third line that the move may be an escape of some kind. The persona emphasizes the godlike (or at least Adam-like) nature of his brother which led him to seek the idyllic life, the innocent life as it is described in the next five lines (5–10).

The country life is equatable with the good life because it is close to nature, where virtuous behavior, innocence, and purity are all *natural*; they are sought not in name only (as, it is implied, happens at court), but because of the "natural" desire of the pastoral man to

11. There has been some debate on the probable sources for this poem. Those most often mentioned are Horace, *Epodes* II; Virgil, *Georgics* II.493–540; and Jonson, "To Sir Robert Wroth" (*The Forest*, iii). None of these poems, however, is close enough to Herrick's in tone, structure, or substance to claim priority as a "source." Horace's epode, for instance, although similar in some details to Herrick's poem, does not treat the city-country opposition to any great extent and does not mention the doctrine of the mean, or moderation, as the basis of pastoral contentment—the very heart of "A Country life." Likewise, Jonson's verse-epistle also lacks the emphasis on moderation and is considerably more urban-oriented than Herrick's. It is also interesting to note that all three "sources" use a seasonal scheme in their structures, whereas Herrick does not. For fuller discussion of all these poems, and of the country-house genre to which all belong, see G. R. Hibbard, "The Country-House Poem of the Seventeenth Century," *Journal of the Warburg and Courtauld Institutes* 19 (1956): 159–74; and Charles Molesworth, "Property and Virtue: The Genre of the Country-House Poem in the 17th Century," *Genre* 1 (1968): 141–57.

live well. The philosophical doctrine underlying this assumption is given in lines 10–15: the circle of perfection is unbroken in the natural realm, for here wisdom and nature go hand in hand; even Astrea remains content. The country man is wise and just simply because he is a part of nature. To a large extent, this wisdom consists of the ability to "confine desires," or the Stoic moderation once again. The brother is content (in line 22 the declaration, "thou art content" is, like the opening invocation, a clear sanctification of him) because he recognizes that ambition and greed are dangerous for the good life, that everything has its "proper stint," and that satisfaction is achieved only when man rids himself of gluttony in all its forms.[12]

Having presented the doctrinal foundations of the poem, the persona goes on to apply them in general terms to the brother's actual country existence by means of a three-part argument based on the idea of peace (or contentment): the country man is at peace with his spouse, whose "married chastity" yields domestic bliss (ll. 31–42); at peace with his surroundings, which provide him with pleasant dreams and cheerful thoughts (ll. 43–54); and at peace with his God, to whom he sacrifices a portion of his rewards each morning (ll. 55–62).

In line 63 the persona returns to the courtly-country opposition and, still speaking in general terms, contrasts the brother's daily activities with those of the city workers. He has no such desperate cares as the merchants who must sail dangerous seas because, having all he desires or needs at home, he is blessed with "securest ease." He is, as the persona implies, content with his lot, and by now the concept strikes us with more force. Contentment is living according to one's means, according to one's station in the Chain of Being, and according to the dictates of wisdom and nature. Such a life is possible only in the country, for "Vice rules the Most, or All at Court."

The next section of the poem (ll. 93–104) presents once more the

12. Paul Jenkins ("Rethinking What Moderation Means to Robert Herrick") argues that the "moderation" of "A Country life" goes far beyond right conduct to "discriminating imagination" (p. 52). That is, once man is freed from the worries of city life, he can revel in the enchantment of "an inner, imagined landscape" (p. 52). The corrective Jenkins provides against interpreting Herrick's "moderation" in too rigid a sense is very welcome, but he perhaps goes too far toward denying ethical interests altogether.

philosophical basis of Herrick's pastoral vision, though this time in slightly altered terms. Fortune, the most oppressive force for the merchants and other city dwellers, is powerless in the country, for the rural man boldly confronts whatever comes, standing "center-like" (again the circle-of-perfection image), indifferent to Fortune's whims. The doctrine here is Stoic and Boethian: "*A wise man ev'ry way lies square.*"[13] Thus, the persona goes on to say, no matter how little or how much the brother is given by fate, he is content; whether it be food (ll. 105–20) or shelter (ll. 121–36), "*Content makes all Ambrosia.*" At the end of the section the reader finds himself where he began: the persona exhorts the brother to "shun the first, and last extreame" (the doctrine of moderation), and to "live round, and close, and wisely true/ To thine owne selfe; and knowne to few." The progression is somewhat similar to that in "His Grange" and "His content in the Country." In this poem, however, the persona provides more support for his final conclusion: because life in the country follows the laws of nature, the country dweller is by definition truer to his own self, to his "natural" and innocent self, to even his Adamic self, than he who chooses to remain at the corrupt court.

Finally, the persona closes with a blessing and an additional exhortation:

> Thus let thy Rurall Sanctuary be
> > *Elizium* to thy wife and thee;
> There to disport your selves with golden measure:
> > *For seldome use commends the pleasure.*
> Live, and live blest; thrice happy Paire; Let Breath,
> > But lost to one, be th'others death.
> And as there is one Love, one Faith, one Troth,
> > Be so one Death, one Grave to both.
> Till when, in such assurance live, ye may
> > Nor feare, or wish your dying day.
>
> > > > (ll. 137–46)

13. Cf. Seneca, "The Sole Good," No. 76, *Letters to Lucilius* (*The Stoic Philosophy of Seneca*, p. 210); and Boethius, *The Consolation of Philosophy*, tr. Richard Green, IV, Prose 7 (New York, 1962), p. 99.

The command to live with "golden measure" is in perfect accord with the Stoic injunctions throughout the poem, but the sudden intrusion of the fact of death comes as a bit of a shock on first reading. In the midst of this "Sanctuary," this *"Elizium,"* come the figures of death and the grave. There is no suggestion that death can in any way be transcended, that some more glorious reward awaits the happy pair. The fact of death is as blatant as the nettles, colworts, and beets. Presumably it is to be met with the same calm acceptance shown these other natural elements. The injunction is again typically Stoic[14] and suggests that commitment to the natural life, to the life of the country and the pastoral vision, entails also a commitment to death itself as one of the inevitable occurrences in the natural cycle. And, given the natural processes as they exist, there is no transcending this obvious end.

The problem which Herrick raises here will ultimately prove to be the major one in his entire pastoral vision. Given the joys of this existence, given the contentment to which it predisposes its adherents, there is still the reality of transience, mutability, and death. In fact, the pastoral probably gives a clearer understanding of the inevitability of death than any other approach because of its commitment to nature. But it does not allow for any transcendence, though it does suggest some possibilities, such as the natural cycle of birth, death, and *rebirth.* Herrick will examine this "escape" at times, but his conclusion is almost always the same: death is an oppressive fact and only some transcendence other than the conventional pastoral ones will prove satisfactory, especially to one, like himself, who is so intimately concerned with this problem. That Herrick's personae are intimately concerned with it will be readily apparent as more of their representative statements are examined and as we discover that virtually all the views of reality they present end with the note of death. That the persona in this poem gives no solution to the problem may indicate that the work is an early exploratory treatment of the pastoral. That is, at this point the persona's concern is not with any "problem" as such; only as the pastoral life is defined in more detail does fact turn into predicament.

14. See Rollin, *Robert Herrick*, p. 42.

"A Country life" does not purport to be an actual representation of pastoral existence in mimetic terms: it is a statement of the value of such a life in opposition to that of the court. The brother and his wife serve, not as a means of dramatizing or visualizing this life, as we might expect in a typical country-house poem, but as mannequins on which the poet drapes his conception of the underlying ethos of such a life. Nevertheless, the poem is ceremonial. It does not question the values of country living, nor does it struggle to integrate this vision with another. The singer-persona (whose voice exists below but concurrent with that of the "brother") does not try to correlate differing views of reality, or even to persuade the reader in any active sense that his view is best. He simply presents his view in such a way that the singing of it is *a priori* a celebration of it. The near sanctification of the brother is one means of achieving this ceremonial character. That is, the singer elevates the significance of the brother as a human being and places him in a similarly heightened environment. Then he amplifies the depicted incidents to give them the appearance of a kind of ritualistic and communal activity, one which is controlled by a precise sequence of events and a completed and self-sufficient unit of action. In this sense, and on this level, even the projected deaths of the brother and his wife are accommodated in the ritual framework as simply the final rite of their existence. The persona leads the reader through the ritual to an intuitive celebration of the pastoral vision. We cannot go so far as to claim that the participation (by both persona and reader) in the pastoral rite is more important than the thesis being presented, for thesis here seems to take precedence. Such is not always the case however.

The second poem in this minor sequence of comprehensive classical-pastoral visions is "The Country life, to the honoured Master Endimion Porter" (H-662). The poem presents the same vision as "A Country life," but provides a more detailed and substantial setting. It opens with the conventional opposition between city and country:

> SWeet Country life, to such unknown,
> Whose lives are others, not their own!

> But serving Courts, and Cities, be
> Less happy, less enjoying thee.
> Thou never Plow'st the Oceans foame
> To seek, and bring rough Pepper home:
> Nor to the Eastern Ind dost rove
> To bring from thence the scorched Clove.
> Nor, with the losse of thy lov'd rest,
> Bring'st home the Ingot from the West.
>
> (ll. 1–10)

The opposition here is made precise by naming the objects for which the merchants risk their lives. "Rough Pepper," "scorched Clove," and "Ingots" represent the "immoderate" desires fostered by the courtly life. And, as if the point were not yet clear, the speaker immediately compares these merchants to Porter:

> No, thy Ambition's Master-piece
> Flies no thought higher then a fleece:
> Or how to pay thy Hinds, and cleere
> All scores; and so to end the yeere:
> But walk'st about thine owne dear bounds,
> Not envying others larger grounds:
> For well thou know'st, *'tis not th'extent*
> *Of Land makes life, but sweet content.*
>
> (ll. 11–18)

The use of the word "ambition" evokes a whole train of Renaissance associations. Each man, according to the traditional conception of the Chain of Being, is placed in a specific state or hierarchical level to which his personal goals and excellences belong. Ambition is by definition wrong for it implies that one desires to alter his God-ordained position. Any shift in station inevitably disrupts not only the hierarchical structure of society, but the entire universal system. Stretched to its logical conclusion, the breaking of any one link destroys the entire chain. Porter is thus living in accordance with the divine plan because he does not envy others, is not ambitious, and lives a life of "sweet content." Once more the philosophical implications of contentment expand—now to include heaven's Providence.

From this point on the poem divides into roughly two sections: the first, lines 19–45, describes a typical day in Porter's life, complete with exemplary acts (treading his fields, smelling the blossoms, examining the flocks), and interspersed with aphoristic *sententiae* (". . . the best compost for the Lands/ Is the wise Masters Feet, and Hands"; "The Kingdoms portion *is the Plow*"; "Thou seest a present God-like Power/ Imprinted in each Herbe and Flower"). The second part, lines 46–69, presents a new aspect of the country life. "For Sports, for Pagentrie, and Playes," Porter has his choice of a wide variety of pastoral activities: dances, wakes, quintels, shearing feasts, harvest-home festivals, games, revellings, hunts, and so forth. Though the depiction is limited to a simple list, it is still more specific than the pastoral persona has been to this point, and he is closer here perhaps to the domestic voice. Thematically, the poem represents, in relation to "A Country life," the same kind of progression which could be argued in the *Hesperides* as a whole: the presentation first of the philosophical principles upon which an evaluation of the pastoral life is based, then an application of those principles to actual domestic situations.[15] Thus, the implicit contentment and joy of the country life presented in general terms in the opening sections of the poem are, in this second part, given actuality by the detailed celebratory activities.

15. The problem of order in the *Hesperides* has plagued all of Herrick's critics. Some dismiss it by claiming there is no logic to the order and that Herrick was indifferent to the whole matter (Moorman, *Robert Herrick*, p. 28); some attempt subtle and elaborate schematic arrangements to explain its logic (Ross, " 'A Wilde Civilitie'," pp. 182ff.); while still others claim a "deliberate confusion" (Delattre, *Robert Herrick*, pp. 482–87). Kimmey's "Order and Form in Herrick's *Hesperides*" is the latest contribution to the debate. Delattre's "deliberate confusion" seems the most acceptable approach with three important qualifications: (1) that this "confusion" may be more experiment than uncertainty, for the thematic progression of the volume as a whole would seem to be from tentative exploration to more conclusive resolution; (2) that this "confusion" may be similar to and owe something to that in Catullus' *Carmina*; and (3) that the "deliberateness" of the confusion can be understood only by coming to grips with the volume as a whole first, and especially with Herrick's apparent delight in juxtaposing poems of differing genres, tones, and personae.

The final six lines of the poem summarize what has gone before:

> O happy life! if that their good
> The Husbandmen but understood!
> Who all the day themselves doe please,
> And Younglings, with such sports as these.
> And, lying down, have nought t'affright
> Sweet sleep, that makes more short the night.
> *Caetera desunt*—

The "Sweet sleep" of the final line is an emblematic summation of the contentment of the country man and as such draws the reader's attention back to the level of thesis-presentation to which it was directed in the opening sections of the poem. The concluding statement that the poem is unfinished could be argued against structurally. The poem has gone as far as possible in this particular form and this particular mode: the persona has presented the thesis, demonstrated it through specific illustrations, and finally returned to a restatement of it. Any further exploration would be superfluous and would jeopardize the unity of the poetic whole. All expectations are fulfilled; the poem is effectively "closed."[16]

Several features of this poem take it beyond "A Country life." For one thing, it is more mimetic. It still presents a thesis, but that thesis is given poetic actuality by being visualized in terms of a specific action, in this case a chronological daily routine. The interesting point, however, is not simply the mimetic character of the poem, but the ritualistic nature of the action imitated. The day depicted is not an

16. See Barbara Herrnstein Smith, *Poetic Closure* (Chicago, 1968) for a discussion of "framing" as a closural device for poems having a paratactic structure—that is, ones in which repetition is the basic principle of thematic generation, or which rely on lists or variations on a theme. Here the "sweet sleep" and the reference to night serve as closural forces both in terms of effecting the necessary frame (by metaphorically reinvoking the idea of "contentment") and in terms of what Smith calls "terminal motion" (pp. 98–102; 177–78). It might be added that this book is invaluable for any full-scale formalistic analysis of Herrick's verse because it provides a language in which one can discuss the effectiveness of his perfect sense of timing—when to change direction and when to simply end.

ordinary one, but a carefully controlled and ordered one; each step
Porter takes is turned into a miniature rite. For instance, in lines 19–
24, the literal action is no more than Porter walking in his cornfield,
but that act is given more significance than it would normally have:
". . . the best compost for the Lands/ Is the wise Masters Feet, and
Hands." The aphoristic *sententia* demonstrates that Porter, in walking
his lands, insures in some way a successful harvest. The point is similar
to that in "A good Husband" (H-771): "where/ He sets his foot, he
leaves rich *compost* there" (ll. 7–8). The act of walking becomes a
ritualistic communion with nature in which both participant and object
are enriched. It is the ceremonial, the performance of the ritual, which
effects this communion.

In the same way the penultimate section of the poem turns the
"enjoyment" of the pastoral life into another form of ritualistic
activity. In this case, the persona does not describe just what the
harvest-home entails, or what the Christmas revellings are, but is
content merely to show that the joy which Porter receives from his
country living is connected with or dependent upon these small ritualistic acts. Each one celebrates some aspect of the pastoral vision and
each is, therefore, a small ceremonial complete in itself; taken together, as the appositive listing suggests, they represent the larger
festive rite of pastoral "enjoyment."

The poem presents, then, a persona singing about the ritualistic
nature of the pastoral world. But his singing is itself ceremonial. It
is, especially in the penultimate section, quite similar to "The Argument." The choice to "sing" these rites involves making a judgment
on them, and that judgment necessarily involves a poetic statement of
their ultimate value. The "singing" and the "song" are in this sense
ceremonial. The poem perhaps goes a step beyond the ceremonial
nature of "The Argument" by providing the philosophical basis upon
which the value judgment is made and, as a result, it celebrates not
simply the individual activities of the pastoral life, but the entire
pastoral vision. In addition, the mode of ceremonial presentation is
such that we, as readers, are asked to respond in the same fashion: we

are asked to acknowledge the value of these rituals and to celebrate them along with the speaker of the poem.

"A Paranaeticall, or Advisive Verse" (H-670) is distinguished from the two preceding poems by making even more explicit the major qualification of the pastoral life as the classical persona sees it. The poem opens with an exhortation in the familiar Stoic fashion to live moderately. It is true, says the speaker, that the country life demands a certain amount of work, but that work should be conducted "Although with some, yet little paine." He reminds Wicks (Master John Wicks, to whom the poem is addressed), that "*Jove* decrees/ Some mirth, t'adulce mans miseries." The emphasis upon mirth versus misery, on little sweat and little pain, suggests a quite different application of the moderation principle. An inkling of the direction in which the persona is moving appears when he begins, in terms roughly analogous to the Thomas Herrick poem, to speak of Wicks' wife. He urges Wicks to enjoy "Those minutes, Time has lent us here," to live freely and comfortably "while Fates suffer." The emphasis seems more Epicurean than in the other two poems of this group. The final eighteen lines clarify the nature of the persona's appeal:

> Time steals away like to a stream,
> And we glide hence away with them.
> *No sound recalls the houres once fled,*
> *Or Roses, being withered:*
> Nor us (my Friend) when we are lost,
> Like to a Deaw, or melted Frost.
> Then live we mirthfull, while we should,
> And turn the iron Age to Gold.
> Let's feast, and frolick, sing, and play,
> And thus lesse last, then live our Day.
> *Whose life with care is overcast,*
> *That man's not said to live, but last:*
> *Nor is't a life, seven yeares to tell,*
> *But for to live that half seven well:*
> And that wee'l do; as men, who know,

Some few sands spent, we hence must go,
Both to be blended in the Urn,
From whence there's never a return.

(ll. 22–39)

We are suddenly face to face with the problem raised only cursorily in the Thomas Herrick poem. The commitment to the pastoral life, with its emphasis upon contentment and moderation on the one hand, and acting in accordance with the laws of nature on the other, also commits one to a view of death as the inevitable, natural, and life-concluding act. The statement which the persona gives here is both typical and classical: it is the conventional *carpe diem* argument of the Epicureans at its most theoretical level. Time steals away; nothing in the natural realm is static; all is transient and, in the long run, perishing. The *carpe diem* resolve to seize the day is given greater urgency by the recognition of the fleeting nature of time. The persona emphasizes this injunction by imploring that he and Wicks live "mirthfull," that they "feast, and frolick, sing, and play." They may not be able to stop the ever-receding gyre of time, but they can "turn the iron Age to Gold"—essentially the same protest which the persona of Marvell's "To His Coy Mistress" makes:

Thus, though we cannot make our Sun
Stand still, yet we will make him run.

(ll. 45–46)[17]

But whereas Marvell in this poem, and the Cavaliers in most of theirs, end on a positive or at least affirmative assertion of the "seizing" force which man *can* exert, Herrick does not let his persona, Wicks, or the reader off so easily. The conclusion is the same as that in "A Country life": death is the end, final and irrevocable, of all existence, and can in no way be transcended:

Both to be blended in the Urn,
From whence there's never a return.

17. *The Poems and Letters of Andrew Marvell*, ed. H. M. Margoliouth, I (Oxford, 1967), p. 27.

It is once more the Stoic resolve to face death with calm acceptance, to see it as simply one more fact of life, or the process of life, which must be taken in stride.

"A Paranaeticall" thus provides a curious combination of Stoic insistence on passive resignation to death and Epicurean insistence on seizing and enjoying the most that one can in the present. "Curious" may be the wrong word here, for certainly there is nothing unique in combining these two approaches—in fact, we rarely find a philosophical (as opposed to a purely seductional) treatment of the *carpe diem* motif in either classical or English verse which does not take both injunctions into account. What is curious, however, is that most poems in the convention do not lay such a firm foundation for the pastoral commitment. Once this is done, once the persona has totally aligned himself with the pastoral way of life, he has no escape from the inevitability and finality of death. For this reason, the Epicurean *carpe diem* injunction seems a more futile effort in the face of the facts of pastoral existence and brings to these Stoic "contentment" poems a seriously discordant and anxious tone.

Furthermore, a closer examination of the poem indicates that Herrick is very careful to slow the speed of the final eighteen lines by emphasizing only the long vowel sounds and is altogether more somber here than in the first section of the piece. The rhetorical questions of the earlier part do not appear in this one; all references to joy or pleasure are immediately qualified by the sobering thought of death; and the persona becomes, in opposition to that of the two preceding poems, a pleader. All suggests another instance of tone belying statement. The pastoral vision, and perhaps its festive rites as well, are seriously qualified.

Two poems in which Herrick takes up this qualification in particular are "To Meddowes" (H-274) and "To Blossoms" (H-467). The first treats time and death by means of a meditation on a natural object:

> YE have been fresh and green,
>   Ye have been fill'd with flowers:

And ye the Walks have been
  Where Maids have spent their houres.

You have beheld, how they
  With *Wicker Arks* did come
To kisse, and beare away
  The richer Couslips home.

Y'ave heard them sweetly sing,
  And seen them in a Round:
Each Virgin, like a Spring,
  With Hony-succles crown'd.

But now, we see, none here,
  Whose silv'rie feet did tread,
And with dishevell'd Haire,
  Adorn'd this smoother Mead.

Like Unthrifts, having spent,
  Your stock, and needy grown,
Y'are left here to lament
  Your poore estates, alone.

In the first stanza the speaker presents the situation and defines the meadows. The time is past: the meadows *have been* fresh and green, and filled with flowers; because of this, they have also been filled with maidens. The function, it seems, of the meadows is to provide a setting in which the May-rites can occur, as the next two stanzas explain. The *"Wicker Arks"* bearing "Couslips," the sweet singing and dancing of a round, and the wearing of "Hony-succle" crowns are all associated with the May Day rituals. Like stanza one, the second and third are in the past tense, suggesting that the element of time is somehow the agent bringing the human and the natural realms together. Lines 11–12 enforce this point:

  Each Virgin, like a Spring,
    With Hony-succles crown'd.

The eleventh line establishes a metaphoric relationship between "Virgin" and "Spring": the virgin is like the spring in terms of freshness, liveliness, loveliness, and adornment. The metaphor functions to incorporate the human into the natural. In terms of both lines, however, "Spring" functions also as a phase of the time-sequence, distinct from the metaphor of line 11. Thus, the position of "Spring" midway between "Virgin" and "Hony-succles" serves to bind the two realms implied by these terms together into a state of "Spring-ness." Time is the controlling element uniting what are otherwise distinct aspects of existence.

In the fourth stanza the poem suddenly shifts its time scheme. "But now, we see, none here." The human and natural realms have been divorced and the meadow is left lamenting *alone*. The placing of this final word, and the heavy caesural pause before it, are effective in underscoring the total separation which has *now* occurred.

The thesis here gives a new twist to the problem of transience. In the first place, it demonstrates that time can be a synthesizing force, but paradoxically, the union created by time is inevitably destroyed by it also. The very process which gives rise to a unity of existence dooms that unity to irrevocable dissolution.

In "To Blossoms" Herrick deals with the same problem:

> FAire pledges of a fruitfull Tree,
>   Why do yee fall so fast?
>   Your date is not so past;
> But you may stay yet here a while,
>   To blush and gently smile;
>   And go at last.
>
> What, were yee borne to be
>   An houre or half's delight;
>   And so to bid goodnight?
> 'Twas pitie Nature brought yee forth
>   Meerly to shew your worth,
>   And lose you quite.

But you are lovely Leaves, where we
May read how soon things have
Their end, though ne'r so brave:
And after they have shown their pride,
Like you a while: They glide
Into the Grave.

The persona here is perhaps more firmly intrenched in the planctus tradition than the speaker of the preceding poem, but he begins at the same point: the presentation of and meditation on a natural object. And, like the former's, his meditation leads to a new awareness about the situation and the value of the object. He begins by lamenting the passage of time which forbids a longer "date" for the "Faire pledges." The blossoms are "pledges" because they are the bearers of new trees and hence the means of continuing the cyclic pattern of birth, death, and rebirth. But the emphasis in the poem is almost exclusively on the middle phase of this cycle. The theme of the first stanza is therefore equivalent to Daniel's "Short is the glory of the blushing Rose" (*Delia*, XLII, 6)¸ and echoes the Renaissance artist's typical aesthetic complaint that beauty is by definition shortlived.[18]

The second stanza continues the complaint and makes explicit the persona's concern with the middle phase of the natural process rather than the final one. The note on which he ends is that the death of the blossoms is a complete loss: "lose you quite." The implicit rebirth is negated, for even that would not reproduce the same form of blossom. The cause of the loss is assigned specifically to Nature, who brings forth the blossom "Meerly to shew [her] worth." By using the word "Meerly" the persona seems to be saying that aesthetic ends are not enough, that the blossom should have a more significant function. That it does he momentarily forgets.

The third stanza gives what amounts to a "romantic" reading of the blossom's significance as the natural object presents the "seer" with a specific correspondence between the natural and the human

18. See Haydn, *The Counter-Renaissance*, pp. 361–69.

realms of existence. All things are destined for the same end: "They glide/ Into the Grave." The metaphoric and emblematic meaning of the blossoms is completed as the speaker laments, through the literal natural object, the fleeting "date" of all existence. Time, as a natural process, leads everything to the one inevitable end. The classical-pastoralist's commitment to nature and the natural process demands, as said before, a commitment also to the finality of death. The mere fact that we find this persona in the role of a lamenting observer suggests an important qualification on the pastoral vision (with its Stoic emphasis on passive acceptance) as he presents it.

ii. The Domestic Voice

Since the domestic-pastoral persona proceeds from essentially the same philosophical bases as the classical one, it is unnecessary to repeat them here. Of more importance is the manner in which he demonstrates the joys of the country life by using specific situations and precise details—by writing, that is, primarily mimetic lyrics in which the major appeal is to a "felt" experience. Rather than the generalized and unlocalized depictions of the classical persona, this one gives us exact manifestations of the significance of the pastoral vision as embodied in daily life. Furthermore, the main concern of the domestic persona is with the sheer joy of the country life in all its various forms. He is not concerned to argue a thesis and is less interested in analyzing or understanding the joy of the good life than in merely imitating it. Consequently, his poems tend to deal with rather simple festive and dramatic occasions during which the true pastoral joys are clearly evident.

The most representative poem of this class is "The Hock-cart, or Harvest home" (H-250). The poem is constructed of four parts: the first section (ll. 1–6) is an invitation to the festivities; the second (ll. 7–25) presents the actual festival itself; the third (ll. 26–43) outlines the food and drink which the lord of the manor has provided for the occasion; and the fourth (ll. 44–55) is an exhortation to the workers to approach this moment of respite in the proper frame of mind. The opening invitation is given in the following terms:

> COme Sons of Summer, by whose toile,
> We are the Lords of Wine and Oile:
> By whose tough labours, and rough hands,
> We rip up first, then reap our lands.
> Crown'd with the eares of corne, now come,
> And, to the Pipe, sing Harvest home.
>
> (ll. 1–6)

Besides inviting the "Sons of Summer" to participate in the hock-cart festival, the passage also defines these "Sons" as the laborers, the workers of the field, the reapers of the corn. They are to be distinguished from the "Lords of Wine and Oile"—the "we" of the second and fourth lines. The latter are the landlords ("our lands") and include the persona. While the concern with drawing this distinction is perhaps not understandable at this point in the poem, the division proves necessary both structurally and thematically.

The second section (7–25), addressed specifically to Mildmay Fane, the chief landlord, begins:

> Come forth, my Lord, and see the Cart
> Drest up with all the Country Art.

The nature of this invitation and its juxtaposition to that of the "Sons" in the preceding lines serve to clarify the importance of the distinction made earlier. The lord's participation is not quite the same as the "Sons'," for his is a more vicarious enjoyment. His participation is no less valid and essential, however, for despite the separation of ranks made in the first section, the rhetorical device of describing the various actions of the rustics in an address to the lord serves to draw the two classes back together. The lord celebrates the activity through his very presence; his role is that of provider and overseer, as well as sanctifier of the proceedings.

The third section (26–43) carries the separation-unification motif even further. The addressed party is now the "Sons" and the invitation is to the "Lords Hearth." As in the preceding section, the celebration itself brings the "Sons" and the lord together in the festive occasion. The final line of this part ("Drink frollick boyes, till all be blythe") refers to the "Merryment" in line 24 of the address to the lord and clarifies the precise nature of the union of classes effected here—it is a festive, celebratory one. The hock-cart provides a time and a place when the lord and his workers can celebrate together. Or, to state the theme another way, the harvesting ritual functions as a unifying activity; the means of unification is the expression of merriment and joy occasioned by participation in the rite.

The final section of the poem, the exhortation to the "Sons," takes us in one sense away from the ceremony proper. As the lines have been the source of some critical debate,[19] perhaps a closer examination is necessary:

> Feed, and grow fat; and as ye eat,
> Be mindfull, that the lab'ring Neat
> (As you) may have their fill of meat.
> And know, besides, ye must revoke
> The patient Oxe unto the Yoke,
> And all goe back unto the Plough
> And Harrow, (though they'r hang'd up now.)
> And, you must know, your Lords word's true,
> Feed him ye must, whose food fils you.
> And that this pleasure is like raine,
> Not sent ye for to drowne your paine,
> But for to make it spring againe.

> (ll. 44–55)

---

19. The seminal essay in this debate is Robert Lougy's "Herrick's 'The Hock-cart, or Harvest Home,' 51–5," *Explicator* 23 (1964): 13. Lougy's main point is that the lines imply a "sense of indignation and the awareness of injustice," and thus are "critical of the very lord to whom it [the poem] is directed." The most trenchant attack on this position is Roger Rollin's "Missing 'The Hock-cart': An Explication Re-explicated," *Seventeenth-Century News* 24 (1966): 39–40. See also Paul O. Clark, "Herrick's 'The Hock-cart, or Harvest Home,' 51–55," *Explicator* 24 (1966): 70.

The first thing to notice here is the position in which the speaker places the rustics. Like the "lab'ring Neat" and the "patient Oxe," they are "beasts" of the field. The equation is not necessarily derogatory: the rustics' utilitarian purpose, their station in life, the excellence of their position in the hierarchical Chain—however we want to phrase it—depends upon defining them as the "working" class.[20] It is on this assumption, perfectly traditional, that the entire exhortation is constructed, for the purpose of their station is epigrammatically summarized by: "Feed him ye must, whose food fils you." The final lines re-emphasize the stricture already made and can be paraphrased as follows: "This pleasurable moment of rest which you now enjoy will not be permanent, for you will have to return to work once more." Whether we read "it" (l. 55) as the "paine" (in the sense of "pain of labor" or the capacity to work) or as a referent for "raine," and whether we read "spring" as a verb or a noun, the point is still the same—time is not static, but cyclic. The process leading up to this moment of festivity will have to be relived.

The hock-cart festival is worthy of the poet's praise because it provides a formal occasion for the lords and the rustics to unite in a public act of joyous celebration. The poet demonstrates the nature and significance of that act by isolating it in time and by heightening its ritualistic form. In so doing, however, he also raises a complication, for his expanded vision at the end of the poem "places" the festival within a larger temporal context which emphasizes its chronological limit. By focusing so explicitly on the brevity of the ritualistic moment, on the inevitability of its passing, Herrick seems to qualify the importance of the rite. Similarly, the reader is forced to alter his response to the festival by recognizing its limitations.

Such a qualification at the poem's end points to the recurring dilemma of Herrick's pastoral personae. Given the standard pastoral insistence on the inevitable cyclic process of time, how can the tradition be used to isolate and celebrate individual moments? The somber mood of transitory existence threatens to overshadow the celebration of the poem's attempted stasis. The problem for the poet is further com-

20. Rollin, "Missing 'The Hock-cart,'" p. 39.

pounded by the seemingly paradoxical fact that the *isolation* of any given moment of time can be heightened most easily by pitting it against the controlling temporal process. In the present poem, therefore, Herrick's allusion to the cyclic process of planting, cultivating, and harvesting is one means of isolating and defining the single instant of harvest-home. But here the cyclic qualification seems to outweigh, though it does not totally deny, the attempted stasis.

To an extent, all of Herrick's "songs" stop time at key points of the temporal cycle, points which are of greater value if they are consciously and deliberately celebrated in a formal ritualistic manner. One means of tracing Herrick's progression through the *Hesperides*, therefore, is to note how he learns to use the fact of transience to heighten his poetic stasis rather than to qualify it. Transience is perhaps never finally denied, but it is at least controlled and undercut by the timelessness of the artistic ceremonial.

"A New-yeares gift sent to Sir Simeon Steward" (H-319) is also in the domestic-pastoral vein. Again the persona presents a more or less static moment of celebration which is heightened by the artistic and ceremonial rendering. The poem begins with an eight-line protestation of activities not included in this particular moment:

> NO newes of Navies burnt at Seas;
> No noise of late spawn'd *Tittyries*:
> No closset plot, or open vent,
> That frights men with a Parliament:
> No new devise, or late found trick,
> To read by th'Starres, the Kingdoms sick:
> No ginne to catch the State, or wring
> The free-born Nosthrills of the King,
> We send to you . . .

Recent criticism has demonstrated the risks involved in earlier assumptions about the poet's total lack of concern over, or even notice of, the civil strife surrounding him.[21] Patrick and Martin have carefully noted

---

21. Cf. Delattre, *Robert Herrick*: "Alors que l'Angleterre traversait une des périodes les plus anxieuses qu'elle ait jamais connues, notre poète suivait le cou-

the probable events to which these lines allude, though the fact that they do refer to civil incidents is perhaps not as important as the way in which the references function in the poem as a whole. The speaker goes out of his way to assure Steward that his gift—the poem—has nothing to do with such events. As a "New-yeares gift" the poem urges Steward, as well as the reader, to forget or dismiss those troublesome activities surrounding him and to dedicate himself entirely to a celebration of the specific event described in the remaining lines. What follows, however, is not exactly an event at all, but "a jolly/ Verse crown'd with *Yvie*, and with *Holly*." Just how this "jolly Verse" is made a literal event demonstrates one facet of the art of poetic ceremonial.

The body of the poem is divided into three sections: first, the speaker "sings" of "Winters Tales and Mirth" (ll. 9–26); second, he asks to be remembered and toasted on this mirthful occasion (ll. 27–36); and third, he exhorts Steward to "Frolick" with a light heart (ll. 37–50). The structure is similar to that in "The Hock-cart" as it progresses from a description of the festival, to an analysis of the nature of the festival, to finally a statement on the proper manner in which to approach the fete.

Lines 9–26, then, "sing" of "Milk-maids," "Christmas sports," "the *Wassell-boule*," "Twelf-tide Cakes," "crackling Laurell," "and such like things . . ." It is the same kind of list seen in "The Country life" and "The Hock-cart," and the same kind of heightened ceremonial. The list of activities creates a scene of ritualistic merriment and mirth. The significance of these relatively simple and essentially pastoral rites is heightened by the contrast with the more urban or courtly intrigues of the first eight lines.

In the third section of the poem (ll. 27–36) the persona momentarily betrays his true identity by allowing the pastoral mask to fall. He is actually a member of the courtly society who has adopted the pastoral guise as an escape from the conflicts of the court—which he

---

rant de la vie ordinaire qui, même dans les moments de crise nationale, semble peu varier, troublée à peine par les échos de l'orage lointain, sans incident dramatique d'aucune sorte, presque sans histoire" (p. 4).

has already detailed, of course, in the opening lines. The betrayal of identity allows the poet to indicate without literally saying it how significant these merry rites are. If he, by just pretending to participate in them, can momentarily escape the troublesome times, how much more effective will they be in taking Steward, who can literally participate in them, beyond these same times?

In the final section of the poem the tone and mood shift once more, and again the shift is emphasized by a further stripping away of the pastoral mask. There is an additional note of urgency in the final exhortation, not only because of the imperative, but because the reader recognizes that the pastoral ceremony has special meaning to this speaker who, by virtue of his courtly position, cannot take part in it, or who can do so only vicariously and imaginatively. Further, this sense of urgency comes by means of the same qualification noted in the other pastoral poems:

> Then as ye sit about your embers,
> Call not to mind those fled Decembers;
> But think on these, that are t'appeare,
> As Daughters to the instant yeare:
> Sit crown'd with Rose-buds, and carouse,
> Till *Liber Pater* twirles the house
> About your eares; and lay upon
> The yeare (your cares) that's fled and gon.
> And let the russet Swaines the Plough
> And Harrow hang up resting now;
> And to the Bag-pipe all addresse;
> Till sleep takes place of wearinesse.
> And thus, throughout, with Christmas playes
> Frolick the full twelve Holy-dayes.
>
> (ll. 37–50)

The significance of these lines lies in the explicit statement of the major opposition to the kind of pastoral enjoyment which the ceremony or festivity of the second section depicts. That opposition, as we have learned to expect in Herrick's pastoral vein, is the fact of mutability. Steward is urged to forget "those fled Decembers" and the "yeare (your cares) that's fled and gon." The implication is that the remembrance of these fleeting "moments" will inhibit in some way the festivity of the present. Likewise, although the speaker uses a traditional *carpe diem* injunction—"think on these," the present moments—he underscores the fact that even this year is only an "instant," that it too will recede into the past. Even the description of the hanging up of the ploughs and harrows emphasizes the temporal progression, for these objects are only "resting," waiting until the moment of festivity passes and they are called upon once more.

In the face of such stern opposition the speaker urges Steward to "Sit crown'd with Rose-buds, and carouse . . ." and to "Frolick the full twelve Holy-dayes." The Epicurean insistence on making the most of the day at hand is coupled with a Bacchanalian ("*Liber Pater*") response to the literal "seizing" of the day. Steward can overcome the facts of time and transience by celebrating, by frolicking and carousing, throughout this special season. In this way, the ceremonial festivities of the second section of the poem take on a double significance: they are important not only in and of themselves, but because they provide a static moment in which man can "seize" the most of the time which is allotted him. Though the domestic persona recognizes that this moment of festivity will pass (the whole qualification of the pastoral vision), the Christmas activities of the rural dweller do provide, if only for a brief "instant," a means of escaping the transience of his existence. The ceremonial is a call to frolic, a call to "sing" and celebrate the significance and the joy of this static moment in time.[22] Once more the recognition of the opposition which time presents emphasizes both the necessity of celebrating and the importance of the celebratory ritual.

We must not be misled, however, into assuming that the persona is offering a definitive escape from the problem of mutability. He clearly understands the limitations of what he is suggesting. Even on the

22. The New Year's season is, of course, a significant time for any poet concerned with mutability and the urgency which the heightened sense of "ending" provides underlies many of Herrick's poems on this occasion. See, for example, H-146B, 476, 784, 785, 787, 892, 893, 980, 1026; and N-60, 96, 97, 98, 102.

poem's literal level, the fact of mutability qualifies, to some extent, the ceremonial activity. But he just as clearly sees that to "sing" of the ritual and the celebration is to participate in them. And this "sing-ing," by virtue of the mode used, is also an exhortation to the reader to join with him. The ceremony is so heightened in importance that the reader can respond only with celebration himself, as Steward must do also. Furthermore, the reader must see that the persona's "song" is itself a ritual having significance on several levels: his celebratory response is both a recognition of these levels and a conscious affirmation of the value of the act of celebrating. The poem becomes, in a literal sense, the ceremonial rite which it describes.

The second major type of domestic-pastoral poem is represented by the most famous of Herrick's works, "Corinna's going a Maying" (H-178).[23] Most of Herrick's passionate shepherd poems (especially

23. The sources and analogues which have been claimed for this poem are far too numerous to include here, but one poem not yet mentioned as a possible analogue, at least to my knowledge, appears in John Dowland's *The First Booke of Songes or Ayres* (1597):

> Come away! come, sweet Love!
> The golden morning breaks;
> All the earth, all the air,
> Of love and pleasure speaks.
> Teach thine arms then to embrace,
> And sweet rosy lips to kiss,
> And mix our souls in mutual bliss:
> Eyes were made for beauty's grace,
> Viewing, rueing, love's long pain,
> Procured by beauty's rude disdain.
>
> Come away! come, sweet Love!
> The golden morning wastes,
> While the sun, from his sphere,
> His fiery arrows casts,
> Making all the shadows fly,
> Playing, staying, in the grove
> To entertain the stealth of love.
> Thither, sweet Love, let us hie,
> Flying, dying, in desire,
> Winged with sweet hopes and heavenly fire.
>
> Come away! come, sweet Love!
> Do not in vain adorn
> Beauty's grace, that should rise
> Like to the naked morn.

"To the Maids to walke abroad" [H-616] and "To Phillis to love, and live with him" [H-521]—both of which are generically related to "Corinna") begin with the speaker's invitation to the mistress and proceed to describe the act or situation to which she is invited. In "Corinna," however, the invitation is repeated throughout as the opening line(s) of each stanza. It thus works more as a refrain than a frame, and serves as both a unifying and an incremental device. In the latter function, each subtle alteration of the invitation prepares for the specific aspect of the May Day celebration developed in that stanza. For example, in stanza two, the invitation immediately associates Corinna with nature and her dress with natural objects:

> Rise; and put on your Foliage, and be seene
> To come forth, like the Spring-time, fresh and greene.

The rest of the stanza develops the human-natural correspondences suggested here. Similarly, in the final stanza, the sudden intrusion of a qualification in the invitation ("while we are in our prime") heightens the note of urgency and the *carpe diem* insistence on the fleeting nature of time.

The speaker in "To Phillis" and "To the Maids" also progresses by means of a clear spatial and temporal order. In the former poem, he "prepares" the mistress by taking her from the court to the country and by focusing sequentially on her bed, her dress, her food, and so forth. "Corinna," however, seems to be working outside (though not oblivious of) both space and time. The moment of the poem's experience is a static one: each stanza simply redefines in slightly altered terms the same precise instant as the others. The clearest indication of this temporal stasis is Herrick's careful control of the verb tenses.

> Lilies on the river's side,
>   And fair Cyprian flowers new-blown,
>   Desire no beauties but their own:
> Ornament is nurse of pride.
>   Pleasure measure love's delight:
>   Haste then, sweet Love, our wished flight!

(quoted from Norman Ault, *Elizabethan Lyrics* [New York, 1960], pp. 242–43. See also Edward Doughtie, ed., *Lyrics from English Airs* [Cambridge, Mass., 1970], pp. 75–76).

Though the speaker suggests a process going on outside them, and though he seems to take us through a considerable period of time in the five stanzas, he and Corinna remain in a continuous present. In the first three stanzas, all of the controlling verbs are in the present tense. The only deviations occur when the speaker refers to the process of celebration in which the natural realm is engaged (for which he uses a past tense) or when he tells Corinna what she can expect when she joins this celebration (for which he logically uses a future tense). In stanza four Herrick contrasts Corinna's condition with the youths' celebration once again by verb tense—present for Corinna; past for the youths. The predominance of the past tense in this stanza suggests that the lovers are missing something which will not wait for them, but they themselves remain in the same static instant. In the final stanza Herrick returns to the present tense, though now significantly altered by the conditional mood. The lovers are still suspended in a continuous present, but the insistence that time will soon force them either to act or to decay becomes the center of focus. Consequently, although Herrick is able to imply both past and future actions, the entire poem remains in one static moment of human experience.

Underlying this temporal stasis, however, is a carefully controlled thematic progression effected by a subtle shifting of image-pattern and subject matter in each consecutive stanza. The first stanza presents the natural scene to which Corinna is invited; it describes the pastoral setting and, to a certain extent, the importance of that setting. The second stanza treats Corinna herself and her relation to the setting. The two stanzas together establish a pattern of expectation for the poem as a whole: that is, we expect it to move back and forth between the natural and the human realms. The next two stanzas confirm this pattern, for the third re-presents the setting of stanza one though it is now significantly altered and made more specific in terms of an exact locale; and the fourth depicts the human counterparts of Corinna, once again in more specific and realistic terms than in stanza two. Finally, the poem is effectively "closed" by subsuming both the natural realms of one and three and the human realms of two and four under the more urgent temporal realm of the concluding stanza.

In addition to this thematic progression, a sequence of shifting image-patterns or correspondences is operative in the poem. Thus, the concern of stanza one is to present nature in human terms; two presents humanity (here Corinna is representative of all men) in natural terms; three depicts the city in human and natural terms; four shows the youths in natural terms; and five presents all in temporal and transient terms. The progression is not, of course, so rigid as this scheme implies, but it generally follows these lines.

The first stanza, then, presents the major images and motifs of the poem:

> GEt up, get up for shame, the Blooming Morne
> Upon her wings presents the god unshorne.
> See how *Aurora* throwes her faire
> Fresh-quilted colours through the aire:
> Get up, sweet-Slug-a-bed, and see
> The Dew-bespangling Herbe and Tree.
> Each Flower has wept, and bow'd toward the East,
> Above an houre since; yet you not drest,
> Nay! not so much as out of bed?
> When all the Birds have Mattens seyd,
> And sung their thankfull Hymnes: 'tis sin,
> Nay, profanation to keep in,
> When as a thousand Virgins on this day,
> Spring, sooner then the Lark, to fetch in May.

The primary function of the stanza is the humanization and deification of the natural objects. The sun is a "god unshorne"; each flower, in worshiping this god, bows "toward the East"; the birds have "Mattens seyd,/ And sung their thankfull Hymnes"—all nature has awakened in order to participate in the religious ceremony "to fetch in May." It is a special day, a unique time in the yearly cycle. The depiction is as robust and full of life as Chaucer's opening lines in the General Prologue to *The Canterbury Tales*. And almost as incongruous as the pilgrims' withdrawal from the reaffirmation of the vitality and goodness of life is Corinna's still sleeping:

> . . . yet you not drest,
> Nay! not so much as out of bed?

The question embodies an element of disbelief. How can she remain
asleep when all life is waking? She is out of accord with the rest of
nature. Because the natural events which are taking place have been
heightened by the speaker to a status of ritual—of, in fact, a May Day
religion—Corinna sins in not participating. She desecrates herself
and the rite by not appearing.

The artistry at work here is extremely sure of itself. The sin and
profanation of which Corinna is accused in lines 11–12 can be sub-
stantiated only by proving that participation in the rite is the correct,
necessary, and religious thing to do. The poem accomplishes this simply
by its presentation of the natural setting: it is so heightened, so sanctified and ritualized, that to be out of accord with what is happening
within it is to be automatically at fault.

There is one other feature of this opening stanza which bears notice
—the tendency of the poet to deal in correspondences, as already seen
in the personifications of sun, morning, birds, and flowers. But Herrick
also links the human and natural realms by describing the colors of
the morning as "Fresh-quilted"—a patchwork of hues sewn together
to make one "covering" for the entire natural scene. The metaphor
suggests that since nature has risen from its bed, Corinna must do the
same. All the personifications of the stanza function in this manner:
they draw together the various levels of existence. In each case, the
vehicle effecting the union of correspondence is the time in which the
poem is set, for time governs the actions upon which these correspondences are based. And that time is, once again, one of celebration and
ritual.

The speaker moves on in stanza two to define this ritual more
precisely.

> Rise; and put on your Foliage, and be seene
> To come forth, like the Spring-time, fresh and greene;
>   And sweet as *Flora*. Take no care
>   For Jewels for your Gowne, or Haire:

Feare not; the leaves will strew
Gemms in abundance upon you:
Besides, the childhood of the Day has kept,
Against you come, some *Orient Pearls* unwept:
Come, and receive them while the light
Hangs on the Dew-locks of the night:
And *Titan* on the Eastern hill
Retires himselfe, or else stands still
Till you come forth. Wash, dresse, be briefe in praying:
Few Beads are best, when once we goe a Maying.

It is not yet too late for Corinna to join in the devotion; in fact, time has momentarily stood still for her. Through a subtle shift of emphasis she becomes not so much the devotee who must come to worship, but the real object of everyone else's worship. Nature is waiting to praise Corinna as the goddess of May. She is not only "sweet as *Flora*"; she *is* Flora.

Turning Corinna into a May-goddess is not just a trick of the metaphoric pen or a wanton transfer of correspondence. Herrick is working very deliberately here. Corinna's clothes are "foliage"; she comes forth "fresh and greene"; the gems of her hair and her gown are "leaves," or dew drops. These images all function to make Corinna a natural object, to unite her imagistically with the natural realm. When we remember that the natural objects of the first stanza were personified in order to unite them imagistically with the human realm, we begin to grasp Herrick's artistry. The situation has been reversed, but the result is the same: the human and natural realms are united in one specific ritual "to fetch in May."[24]

Herrick continues the metaphoric correspondences in the stanza by

24. It is instructive to compare the correspondences Herrick draws in these first two stanzas with the discussion of tree worship in Sir James Frazer's *The Golden Bough* (New York, 1951), pp. 126–56. Frazer describes both the practice of dressing humans in leaves and flowers on May Day and the anthropomorphic conception of various elements of the natural realm, as well as the correspondences these two tendencies give rise to. In general, Frazer's study provides an excellent gloss to what is probably Herrick's own conception of the May Day festival, or at least of that festival as it appears in this poem.

referring to the "childhood" of the day, by the personification of night with gems of light hanging in her hair, and by the personification of Titan resting on the eastern hill. All of these correspondences demonstrate the total interdependence and interpenetration of the various realms of existence. Corinna is an essential part of the May Day rite because that rite consists of the union of all elements in one moment of unqualified celebration. The picture presented is quite similar to that in Chaucer's *Parlement of Foules*.[25] In that poem, nature is seen as a combination of human and animal, divine and earthly. The portrait here is roughly the same and the profanation occasioned by Corinna's refusal to participate is consequently a double one. Like Chaucer's "tersel egle," she profanes herself by not "completing" herself, by not taking part in the ultimate union of all creation; likewise, because she is absent, the celebration in which the rest of nature participates is not completed either, and she profanes it, too. She does not allow it to fulfill its function of total ritualistic union, for she, as the necessary human agent, refuses to come forth.

In the third stanza, the speaker returns to the natural description which he began in the first, but this time his references are more specific:

> Come, my *Corinna*, come; and comming, marke
> How each field turns a street; each street a Parke
>   Made green, and trimm'd with trees: see how
>   Devotion gives each House a Bough,
>   Or Branch: Each Porch, each doore, ere this,
>   An Arke a Tabernacle is
> Made up of white-thorn neatly enterwove;
> As if here were those cooler shades of love.
>   Can such delights be in the street,
>   And open fields, and we not see't?

25. Chaucer's depiction of the St. Valentine's Day ritual, the coming together of all realms of existence in order to participate in this rite, the definition of love as the ruling force of all creation, the disruption of the ceremony because one necessary member fails to participate properly, and the elevation of love to an essentially religious act—all these features of *The Parlement* find their counterparts in "Corinna."

> Come, we'll abroad; and let's obay
> The Proclamation made for May:
> And sin no more, as we have done, by staying;
> But my *Corinna*, come, let's goe a Maying.

Man-made objects are turned into natural ones as houses and streets
become boughs, branches, fields, and parks. The unification achieved
by the correspondences of the first two stanzas is extended here to
towns and cities as well. There is no courtly-country opposition in
this pastoral vision: all is subsumed in nature. Literally, the stanza
simply presents a picture of the May Day decorations, but the images
function metaphorically to suggest that even in the more courtly
setting the festive ritual unites all objects in one complete and ordered
existence.[26]

Beyond this, the stanza demonstrates again Herrick's concern to
heighten the ritual he is depicting. Thus, the houses are not only natural objects, but religious arks and tabernacles. This fact is more significant than it first appears, for it implies that man need not be in any
specific "place" to achieve the kind of vision to which the poem invites
us. Rather, that particular vision is dependent upon the individual's
perception and time itself. Therefore, when the speaker asks,

> Can such delights be in the street,
> And open fields, and we not see't?

he is positing a legitimate question. A unified and multi-leveled existence surrounds man; all he need do is "see't." In this sense, the
"Proclamation made for May"[27] is important in terms of its extra-
literal implications. It suggests that the exhortation to celebrate and
to commune with all of creation is a natural one, common to and felt

---

26. Cf. Cleanth Brooks's judgment that "the town has disappeared and its
mores are superseded" (*The Well Wrought Urn*, 4th ed. [New York, 1965],
p. 70). Perhaps it would be more accurate to say that the point of the stanza is
not the country "invading" the city, or pastoral mores "superseding" urban
ones, but rather the coming together of both city and country in the unity afforded by the religious and poetic rite.

27. See Patrick's note on this line for the historical context (*Complete Poetry*,
p. 100).

by all men at this time. Chaucer provides a convenient analogue to this conception of the spring rites as almost a universal moral law:

> For May wole have no slogardie a-nyght.
> The sesoun priketh every gentil herte,
> And maketh hym out of his slep to sterte,
> And seith, "Arys, and do thy observaunce."
> ("The Knight's Tale," ll. 1042–45)[28]

And the proclamation must be obeyed: to refuse to participate in this rite is a denial of one's essential humanity and a profanation of the entire order of things. It is for this reason that, after re-emphasizing the religious significance of the occasion, the speaker repeats his injunction: "And sin no more, as we have done, by staying" (his use of *we* here implies additional guilt: Corinna has now caused him to sin as well).

The fourth stanza describes the actual events of the May Day festival. The references are all associated with "those cooler shades of love" mentioned in line 36, for May Day is, both in folk-myth and in the underlying conception of this poem, the day of sacred love and marriage.[29] Herrick's emphasis here is therefore on youth, the May games, and the plighting of troth:

> There's not a budding Boy, or Girle, this day,
> But is got up, and gone to bring in May.

28. Quoted from *The Complete Works of Chaucer*, ed. F. N. Robinson, 2nd ed. (Boston, 1957).

29. Once again Frazer provides the most convenient summary of this conception. Speaking of the annual marriage of Dionysus and his queen, he says: "The object of the marriage can hardly have been any other than that of ensuring the fertility of the vines and other fruit-trees of which Dionysus was the god. Thus both in form and meaning the ceremony would answer to the nuptials of the King and Queen of May" (*The Golden Bough*, p. 165). Later, while describing the sacred marriage of Jupiter and Juno, the marriage wedding all elements of creation (and, we might note, the marriage celebrated in Rome by the Flamen Dialis and his wife, the Flaminica—to whom Herrick also writes concerning a special day of love and of the need for expiating a sin [H-539]), Frazer concludes: "In the England of our day the forests have mostly disappeared, yet still on many a village green and in many a country lane a faded image of the sacred marriage lingers in the rustic pageantry of May Day" (p. 175).

> A deale of Youth, ere this, is come
> Back, and with *White-thorn* laden home.
> Some have dispatcht their Cakes and Creame,
> Before that we have left to dreame:
> And some have wept, and woo'd, and plighted Troth,
> And chose their Priest, ere we can cast off sloth:
> Many a green-gown has been given;
> Many a kisse, both odde and even:
> Many a glance too has been sent
> From out the eye, Loves Firmament:
> Many a jest told of the Keyes betraying
> This night, and Locks pickt, yet w'are not a Maying.

The importance of the stanza lies in the transition from the more abstract pleading of the first three stanzas to the exuberant reality of the literal May Day events: white-thorn gathering, the making of cakes and cream, the "rites" of the youths. It is a time of love, of "cleanly-Wantonnesse"; the activities are essentially and openly wanton and sportive, acts of vibrant love and celebration. The speaker records them with a sense of humor not immediately apparent in the rest of the poem.

The sudden "realism" here prepares for the more profound realism of the final stanza by presenting, in a typically medieval manner, a moment of active and cathartic enjoyment before the sobering thought of mutability is allowed to intrude.[30] That is, it presents a mimetic illustration of the vision given in the first three stanzas: the oneness of all creation can be experienced through the intuitive response of the youths. They feel that oneness, they sense the special nature of the day and the season, and they respond with appropriate celebration and festivity. It is this type of action to which Corinna is invited, though

30. The medieval example which comes easiest to mind is Malory's tale of "The Healing of Sir Urry," in which the reader is given a climactic pause, a cathartic moment of integration and virtue rewarded before being thrown headlong into the swift and total destruction of the Round Table in the final book of the *Morte d'Arthur*. The device is not peculiar to Malory, however, as it functions in similar fashion in several episodes of the *Beowulf* and in Book III of *Troilus and Criseyde*.

the mere fact that she needs to be invited is a qualification on her sensibility. The invitation is to join the coupling of all creation into one united realm of existence—a marriage, as it were, effected by the May Day rites.

The final stanza, then, presents a sudden shift in tone and direction, as well as a more powerful injunction to obey the "Proclamation made for May."

> Come, let us goe, while we are in our prime;
> And take the harmlesse follie of the time.
>> We shall grow old apace, and die
>> Before we know our liberty.
>> Our life is short; and our dayes run
>> As fast away as do's the Sunne:
> And as a vapour, or a drop of raine
> Once lost, can ne'r be found againe:
>> So when or you or I are made
>> A fable, song, or fleeting shade;
>> All love, all liking, all delight
>> Lies drown'd with us in endlesse night.
> Then while time serves, and we are but decaying;
> Come, my *Corinna*, come, let's goe a Maying.

Herrick invokes the *carpe diem* theme in all its austerity. The change in tone is so sudden as to be almost shocking after the four-stanza depiction of bursting life and vitality, and especially after the realistic and virile portrait of the preceding stanza. Much of the force of this shock comes by way of the final couplet, in which "Maying," with all of the festive connotations that have been established in the first four stanzas, suddenly takes on a far more sobering meaning by being rhymed with "decaying." The effect is heightened by Herrick's reversing the position of stanza two, where time had momentarily stood still to await Corinna's coming. The sun is now beginning to move again and time beginning to exert control. The stanza gives, therefore, the ultimate injunction for joining in the rite: it is the lovers' last chance; once missed, it is gone forever. The tenuity of the moment is underscored by the conditional qualification of the present-tense verbs and the implication is that the poet has stretched the stasis to its limit—one more stanza and time would inevitably reassert its forward movement in earnest.

"Corinna" is Herrick's most festive and joyous poem: the vitality of life depicted here is unparalleled in the *Hesperides*. The May Day festivities, by the poem's definition a celebration of love and marriage, are heightened in significance to a cosmic ritual of unification. The emphasis is on "seeing" that we are in a special moment of time—a moment in which all the various elements of existence are united in one magnificent song. For the poet, of course, "Corinna's going a Maying" *is* that song. The poem stops momentarily the fleeting passage of time so that this instant of human experience can be analyzed; it constructs and presents the ritual in which we must participate; it defines the importance of that participation; and it brings together in an artistic stasis all elements of creation.

Despite all this festivity, however, the entrance of the figure of death in the final stanza is a blatant qualification of the poem's pastoral vision. Mutability and transience have the final word and the terrifying irony of celebrating while decaying alters the focus of the ceremonial rite. As in the other domestic poems, Herrick's suddenly expanded vision serves the seemingly contradictory purposes of heightening the isolation of the poem's temporal moment and of suggesting the limits to that moment. And again, the sheer force of the latter emphasis threatens the celebratory act. It does not, I think, shatter the ritual stasis of the poem, but it comes close to doing so. Herrick has yet to find a way to exert his artistic control over time without also admitting its destructive force.

Certain questions have been avoided in this reading, namely those concerning the Christian-pagan tensions of the poem and those dealing with the work as a seduction piece. There can be no doubt that at one level the poem aims at "seduction," as most of the passionate-shepherd treatments do. But the formal nature of the poem, and perhaps even elements of its affective nature, cannot be accounted for on these terms alone. Why does Herrick spend so much time on the various levels of correspondence? Why concentrate more on the pastoral depiction than on the *carpe diem* exhortation? Why heighten so thoroughly the entire action to ritualistic form? To say all this is done by a stock pastoral love-swain to convince Corinna that lovemaking is both a natural and a religious rite is to distort the thought. Lovemaking may very well be such a rite, but the reason behind this assertion is more important than its validity. Love is the chain that binds all creation into one unit, however subdivided and hierarchical that unit may be. On May Day, a day set aside specifically to honor this unifying force, the temporal cycle momentarily halts and love brings all the realms of existence together in a unique and open marriage. The union of the lovers is a microcosmic representation of a universal event, not a simple seduction.

The Christian-pagan tensions, oppositions, and reconciliations that some have traced in the poem need a similar perspective.[31] The different allusions can be identified and classified as either pagan or Christian, and it is possible to show how the one elevates or undercuts the other. However, like most of the poems in the *Hesperides*, this one is neither pagan nor Christian. Herrick wants to heighten the experience and uses whatever religious means are available to him. There is no sense of particular religions in the poem; the reader is more aware of simply religion itself. An underlying sense of the oneness of all creation and a feeling for the duty of worship—these are the elements defining the poem's religious attitude. And whatever we choose to call it, that attitude functions in a perfectly clear manner: it heightens and sanctifies the ritual, helps to define the experience as a ritual, and provides additional exhortation for joining in the ritual. We need go no further. The poem succeeds by virtue of its ceremonial mode, not by its use of religious terms and allusions.

This discussion of the domestic-pastoral poems of the *Hesperides* can be concluded by noting very briefly some of the remaining forms

---

31. The most comprehensive analyses of these pagan-Christian tensions are Brooks's essay in *The Well Wrought Urn*, pp. 67–79, and Swardson's *Poetry and the Fountain of Light*, pp. 58–62.

the pastoral appeal takes. "The Wake" (H-761), for instance, presents the same type of ceremonial as "The Hock-cart," even to the point of emphasizing the "rustics'" contentment with the cheapest merriment, their lack of fear, and an anticipation of the continuing cycle of time. "The Wassaile" (H-476), "Ceremonies for Candlemasse Eve" (H-892), and "The Ceremonies for Candlemasse day" (H-893), all depict actual English events heightened in significance by the form of the presentation. In the Candlemasse Eve poem, for example, the use of various trees as religious, symbolic, and commemorative objects effects a union of the human and the natural similar to that in "Corinna."

The most interesting of the remaining poems is a small group including charms, hag poems, and fairy poems. Though seemingly in a class by themselves, these lyrics may be grouped with the domestic-pastoral ones by virtue of the localized and dramatic rendering. The lyrics are charming and delicate, as appealing as they are simple. The persona reduces all problems to their most elementary aspects, and his solutions often consist simply of a faith in the power of goodness to prevail. If man does the right thing, or says the right thing, good will out in the end. The ritualistic form, especially of the charms, itself determines the country dweller's success.

These poems do, however, represent a divergence from the lyric type we have been examining. The major qualification of all Herrick's pastorals, namely the destructive nature of time, is here not mentioned. For this reason, and because of their obviously more fanciful subject matter, these poems are more explicitly escapist than the preceding ones. Frequently, this escape is to a realm of art itself: the lyrics show Herrick consciously playing with poetic form, as seen most clearly in such works as "The Fairie Temple" (H-223).[32] The ceremonial in such poems is close to what I shall call in the final chap-

32. Daniel H. Woodward suggests the ceremonial nature of this poem by noting that "while reducing a human institution to the miniature, the poem also dilates, by means of the comparison, the smallest things of nature and thereby shows their ritualistic value" ("Herrick's Oberon Poems," *Journal of English and Germanic Philology* 64 [1965]: 279).

ter the artistic: the *poetic* re-creation of an action is far more significant than the action itself. In a sense, therefore, these poems effect a bridge between the domestic-pastoral persona and the artistic one.[33]

More than either the classical or the domestic speakers, the artistic persona confronts directly the qualifications of the pastoral vision which they raise. That is, his primary concern is with transience and death, and his primary purpose is to construct a vision of existence in which these facts have meaning. Also, this persona is more concerned with ceremony *per se*. Unlike the others, who often use the ceremony to show the importance of something else (i.e., the thematic subject of the poem), this persona demonstrates that the ceremony is significant in and of itself. While discussion of this persona must wait until Chapter V so that he can be treated in all his guises, not just the pastoral one, some general features of his works may be described. His poems usually fall into one of two classes: the epitaph or the verse instructions concerning his own burial. In each case, there is an obvious confrontation with death itself. The mere number of such poems suggests that this confrontation is an important one to Herrick, for at least 70 of his pastoral poems fit into one or the other of these ceremonial forms. More important for present purposes is the fact that in these poems Herrick uses poetry itself to take him beyond the oppressive reality of death. He creates here artistic stases over which time and death have no control. Our attention is thus turned in these lyrics from narrative rites to strictly poetic rites. Just how this is accomplished, however, will have to await discussion of Herrick's other personae, their intentions and their concerns.

---

33. Edmund Gosse once remarked that the Jonsonian masque exerted an extraordinary influence on Herrick's poetry (*Seventeenth Century Studies* [New York, 1897], p. 129). Gosse was referring to the kind of fairy lore found in poems like "The Fairie Temple." The suggestion, however, has wider implications, for although Herrick's poems are obviously not allegorical in the way a masque is, the poet's conception of the relationship between literal verbal meaning and human significance may be quite similar to that assumed in the masque. In addition, the intention of the masque to include its audience in the literal celebration is equivalent to the ceremonial poet's desire to involve his reader in the particular celebratory rite which he is depicting.

Chapter III

THE COURTLY
CEREMONIAL

ROBERT HERRICK's membership in the figurative "Tribe of Ben" has long been established,[1] and despite current disaffection with dividing seventeenth-century poetry into distinct "schools," Herrick's adoption of specific courtly personae attests to his familiarity with a tradition of Cavalier verse. The general studies of Felix Schelling, L. C. Potts, Douglas Bush, and, more recently, Robin Skelton, Joseph Summers, and Earl Miner have effectively recovered this tradition for the twentieth-century reader and defined its major characteristics.[2] Still, Herrick's own position in relation to the convention needs closer attention, especially regarding the ceremonial mode of his courtly lyrics.

There is a sense, of course, in which any Elizabethan or Jacobean love lyric could be described as ceremonial. All praise and exalt their mistresses and all transform the act of loving into a stylized and public rite. The distinction of Herrick's verse lies mainly in the kind of stylization and the type of ritual involved. The stylization of the later followers of both the Elizabethan and the Cavalier "schools"[3] consists

1. The most comprehensive analysis of Herrick's place in the Cavalier tradition, and still the fullest critical evaluation of the poet, is Floris Delattre's *Robert Herrick*.

2. Bush, *English Literature in the Earlier Seventeenth Century*, pp. 107–29; Potts, "Ben Jonson and the Classical School," *English Studies* 2 (1929): 7–24; Felix Schelling, "Ben Jonson and the Classical School," *Publications of the Modern Language Association of America* 13 (1898): 221–49 and *The English Lyric* (Boston, 1913), pp. 78–93; Skelton, *Cavalier Poets* (London, 1960); Summers, *The Heirs of Donne and Jonson* (New York, 1970); and Miner, *The Cavalier Mode from Jonson to Cotton* (Princeton, 1971).

3. "Elizabethan" and "Cavalier" are here used in a very restricted sense. I am considering the late Elizabethan sonnet sequences as roughly equivalent to the Jacobean love lyric and am thinking of such representative figures as Barnes, Barnfield, Constable, Drayton, Fletcher, and Lodge; by Cavaliers I mean Cartwright, Godolphin, Lovelace, Suckling, and Townshend. These lists omit, of

mainly of the constant reiteration of conventional similes, analogies, motifs, and situations. Their poetry is stylized, in other words, because it is constructed of "stock" material. Similarly, the "ceremonial" involved in the late Elizabethan and late Cavalier verse too often describes the relationship between the poet and his poem, not the resultant form of his artistic treatment. More precisely, this verse can be called ceremonial only in the sense that all the poets write from the same public point of view and deal in the same verse-compliments. It is a ceremony of Elizabethan and Cavalier poetry, not an Elizabethan or Cavalier poetic ceremonial. Unlike Herrick's, their verse-compliments are not in themselves ceremonial in the sense that they create an ordered and integrated celebratory act in which both poet and audience participate. As would-be poetic ceremonials, such lyrics are sterile because they are often recognizably insincere and false, too conventional to involve either the author or the reader. When an essentially public, celebratory poetry reaches such a static and lifeless condition, it must be either reworked completely or discarded in favor of a more relevant and personal mode of expression. The latter is the alternative chosen by Donne; the former, by Herrick.

Some other distinctions may help to clarify these points. First, the focus of the later Elizabethan and Jacobean verse-compliment is not really on the mistress at all, but on the poet himself—on his ingenuity, his wit, at times even his boldness. With Herrick the situation is reversed: the focus is generally on the mistress and the emotions she evokes in her admirer. For this reason, the "reality" of Herrick's mistresses seems greater. Unlike those of the Elizabethans or the Cavaliers, who serve only as narrative mannequins on which the poets drape their ingenious trimmings, Herrick's mistresses have a vitality which allows us to respond to them as actual women, despite the fact that they are not individualized and are therefore interchangeable. Second,

course, the major poets of each "school," but the point is that the later members tend merely to use conventional forms rather than to create new ones. For this reason, although both groups write in what is presumably a ceremonial mode, that mode has lost its essential features by the time we reach these late figures. Cf. A. J. Smith, "The Failure of Love: Love Lyrics after Donne," *Metaphysical Poetry*, ed. Malcolm Bradbury and D. J. Palmer, Stratford-upon-Avon Studies 11 (New York, 1970), pp. 41–71.

this distinction can be seen as a contrast between words and actions, or between dialectics and emotions. Because the Elizabethan and Cavalier poetry focuses on what the poet can say about the mistress, its real subject is the language itself. It does not attempt to present the mistress in a recognizable situation or to validate the emotions it claims she inspires. The simple fact that a Cavalier mistress never falls or has her shoe untied is telling. These are real, human situations which Herrick exploits for their emotional impact and which he transforms into meaningful emblematic acts. They give evidence of a sensibility to actual experience and "felt" emotion, both of which are too often lacking in his Cavalier contemporaries. Herrick revitalizes the ceremonial by making it fulfill its original purpose as a vehicle of form and expression, not merely a set of sterile conventional devices.

Herrick's courtly personae can be distinguished in the same way we separated the guises of the pastoral voice—recognizing again that the resulting categories are not intended as arbitrary boxes but interpretative conveniences. The first voice can be termed the Cavalier wit, the ingenious Courtier. His poems are well-grounded in the "Tribe" conventions and usually consist of word plays, dialectical tricks, clever correspondences and analogies, and a more or less Bacchanalian approach to life in general. He is perhaps closest to the kind of persona found in the poetry of, say, Thomas Carew. The second Cavalier persona is that of the functionary, or, more specifically, the servant of a patron—be it the king, a lord of the realm, or simply a benefactor. This persona's poems are public in much the same way the former's are: they seek to exalt the patron as the courtier's exalt the mistress. The clearest instance of a similar Cavalier persona is that in Ben Jonson's dedicatory epigrams. The final courtly persona is the celebratory artist. His poems are not actually verse-compliments, not even love-lyrics, and they do not attempt to exalt or celebrate any particular person or mistress even though they may be directed to specific individuals. Instead, they focus the reader's attention directly on the poetry itself, and ask that he praise the artistic processes of ceremonial amplifying and ordering which effect it.

Herrick provides a series of poems clearly divorcing himself and his verse from the pastoral tradition, and thereby establishing, at least implicitly, the courtly persona. In a group of five lyrics—"To Dean-bourn, a rude River in Devon" (H-86), "His returne to London" (H-713), "Upon himself" (H-456), "His Lachrimae or Mirth, turn'd to mourning" (H-371), and "Discontents in Devon" (H-51) —he presents the anti-pastoral attitude in its most extreme form. It has been traditional to associate at least the first two of these poems with Herrick's dismissal from his pastorate in 1947 and with his utter rage at the church laity who supported the Puritan ascendancy.[4] Whether this ascription is valid or not, the poems do serve as a clear indication of an anti-rural, anti-pastoral attitude, and the first, "To Dean-bourn," illustrates just how bitter this stance can be:

> *DEan-Bourn*, farewell; I never look to see
> *Deane*, or thy warty incivility.
> Thy rockie bottome, that doth teare thy streams,
> And makes them frantick, ev'n to all extreames;
> To my content, I never sho'd behold,
> Were thy streames silver, or thy rocks all gold.
> Rockie thou art; and rockie we discover
> Thy men; and rockie are thy wayes all over.
> O men, O manners; Now, and ever knowne
> To be *A Rockie Generation*!
> A people currish; churlish as the seas;
> And rude (almost) as rudest Salvages
> With whom I did, and may re-sojourne when
> Rockes turn to Rivers, Rivers turn to Men.

There is a sense of moral outrage here, of indignation against a people who are simply too rural, who are rude, uncivil, and churlish. The indignation gathers momentum as the poem progresses and culminates in the intense pitch of the last eight lines with their emphatic repetitions and dissonant vocatives. Addressing the river in no way lessens the direct assault on the people themselves. Especially interest-

---

4. Martin confidently assigns both poems to 1647 (*Herrick's Poetical Works*, p. xxxviii).

ing is the use of the "impossibilities" motif in the final couplet—interesting because the entire poem is constructed on the assumption that, literally and metaphorically, these inversions have already taken place.

The anti-pastoral nature of the poem's persona is elaborated in the complementary "His returne to London":

> FRom the dull confines of the drooping West,
> To see the day spring from the pregnant East,
> Ravisht in spirit, I come, nay more, I flie
> To thee, blest place of my Nativitie!
> Thus, thus with hallowed foot I touch the ground,
> With thousand blessings by thy Fortune crown'd.
> O fruitfull Genius! that bestowest here
> An everlasting plenty, yeere by yeere.
> O *Place!* O *People!* Manners! fram'd to please
> All *Nations, Customes, Kindreds, Languages!*
> I am a free-born *Roman*; suffer then,
> That I amongst you live a Citizen.
> London my home is: though by hard fate sent
> Into a long and irksome banishment;
> Yet since cal'd back; henceforward let me be,
> O native countrey, repossest by thee!
> For, rather than I'le to the West return,
> I'le beg of thee first here to have mine Urn.
> Weak I am grown, and must in short time fall;
> Give thou my sacred Reliques Buriall.

The magnificent opening lines of this lyric, with their undertone of religious association and significance, establish a clear contrast between country and city, pastoral and courtly. The country was nothing but an "irksome banishment," for the persona insists he is "a free-born *Roman*." The protestation with which the poem ends enforces the persona's view of himself as a true city man or courtier. And, it must be assumed, since he has returned to the city and to the courtly life, he will return also to the "Lyrick verse" he mentions in "His Lachrimae" —to, that is, his courtly function as "The musick of a Feast."

i. THE CAVALIER VOICE

Herrick's courtly poems proper begin with the voice of the Cavalier wit, a persona who makes use of so many conventional motifs that it is hardly possible here to do justice to his range. I have selected, therefore, representative examples from seven of Herrick's most frequently used lyric types: the stock Petrarchan love-situation, the verse-compliment, the dialectical argument, the protestation, the game-lyric, the parting verse, and the advisory lyric. Each of these types, with the possible exception of the game-lyric, is common enough in the Cavalier tradition,[5] but Herrick is able to work originally with the conventional materials to achieve a more vital ceremonial and celebratory form.

The poems which deal with the Petrarchan love-situation present nearly all the basic attitudes of the Cavalier love-lyric. Generally, they either depict the lady herself or describe the nature of the love she inspires. In the first instance, they concentrate on the mistress's power, variability, fickleness, beauty, cruelty, and self-sufficiency. She can effect any change in any man; she is all powerful and almost totally inaccessible. The guiding spirit behind such treatment is, of course, Petrarch. The second instance emphasizes the pseudo-mystical and neo-Platonic side of love—its paradoxes and contradictions, its mysterious ways of entering the lover, and the curious changes it is able to work on him. In each case the lover-poet is simply a vehicle upon which love and the mistress freely work their wills. The specific theme encountered most frequently, therefore, is the lover complaining about the various contradictory states into which love has forced him.

An elementary example of the type is "Upon Love, by way of question and answer" (H-1001). The poem is not a good one, consisting merely of a list of "answers" to the repeated question, "What will love do?" The answers do present, however, all the stock paradoxes of the Petrarchan love situation—"Like, and dislike ye," "Stroake

---

5. Although my survey has been by no means an exhaustive one, John Lyly's "Cupid and Campaspe" is the only prior example of the kind of game-lyric Herrick writes that I could find.

ye to strike ye," "Heate ye to coole ye," "Stock ye to spend ye," "Kisse ye, to kill ye." Each emphasizes the fickle nature of love which is at one moment favorable, the next unfavorable; the lover is like a sounding board on which love plays its various tunes.

"Upon himselfe" (H-490) and "Of Love. A Sonet" (H-73) elaborate these basic conventions. The first is composed of a series of quatrains in which the speaker protests that he could never act like one in love:

> I co'd never seeke to please
> One, or many Mistresses:
> Never like their lips, to sweare
> *Oyle of Roses* still smelt there.
>
> I co'd never breake my sleepe,
> Fold mine Armes, sob, sigh, or weep:
> Never beg, or humbly wooe
> With oathes, and lyes, (as others do).
>
> (ll. 5–12)

The entire poem is a parody of the standard attitudes of the courtly lover and thus presents a conventional portrait of him. That portrait is the same one we see in English verse at least as early as Chaucer. Again, the main point is that the lover is totally controlled by his love.

"Of Love" is a more limited treatment of the tradition:

> HOw Love came in, I do not know,
> Whether by th'eye, or eare, or no:
> Or whether with the soule it came
> (At first) infused with the same:
> Whether in part 'tis here or there,
> Or, like the soule, whole every where:
> This troubles me: but I as well
> As any other, this can tell;
> That when from hence she does depart,
> The out-let then is from the heart.

The poem plays with conventions, here Petrarchan and Platonic. The question of how love enters the lover is of stock interest to all the courtly poets, but despite their attempts to answer the quesion in a multitude of ways, such answers do not constitute serious concerns. They simply allow witty play on one aspect of the love-relationship. Here, of course, the speaker opts for an inversion of the convention to alter the perspective.

There is not much poetic value in these general statements of the Petrarchan vein. Herrick's best verses of the type are those dealing with Cupid (e.g., "The wounded Cupid" [H-139]), for here he can construct precise and limited dramatic scenes. Most of the poems in this category, however, serve only to establish in broad form the Petrarchan base which underlies the other poems of the Cavalier persona.

The largest and perhaps best group of courtly poems spoken through the voice of the Cavalier wit contains the verse-compliments. Some of these are close in treatment to the pastoral poems, especially when they use natural metaphors to emphasize the essential unity of all creation or the inherent oneness of the natural and the human realms. "Upon Julia's Recovery" (H-9) is a good example:

> DRoop, droop no more, or hang the head
> Ye *Roses* almost withered;
> Now streng⁺h, and newer Purple get,
> Each here declining *Violet.*
> O *Primroses*! let this day be
> A Resurrection unto ye;
> And to all flowers ally'd in blood,
> Or sworn to that sweet Sister-hood:
> For Health on *Julia's* cheek hath shed
> Clarret, and Cream commingled.
> And those her lips doe now appeare
> As beames of *Corrall,* but more cleare.

The poem is obviously courtly in its intentions, but it does make use of the same natural-human correspondences found in the pastorals.

And, as in the country poems, both the natural and human realms are heightened by the religious imagery: the function of the "Sister-hood" of flowers is to beautify the lips and cheeks of the madonna-like Julia. In the final lines, however, the correspondence which the poet has so carefully prepared seems to dissolve as his attention turns to claret, cream, and coral. Claret and cream, though, are images further defining the color of the flowers, which, in turn, define the color of Julia's cheek; they are not used as "things." The beams of coral are somewhat different. In addition to being an image of color (which is probably the main intention since the emphasis is on the beams), the coral implies a solidity, which is, at first glance, inappropriate to the tenor of the poem. It can be argued, however, that the progression of the lyric is from a delicacy in the floral imagery to a crisp hardness in the coral image in order to suggest that Julia's renewed health has somehow taken her beyond the changes and illnesses to which all delicate things are subject. Conversely, the final image could imply a qualification in the compliment: although Julia's lips now *appear* as coral, they are actually flesh and will decay, whereas coral, being solid, will not.[6] This qualification is expanded and clarified in other verse-compliments, such as "To Dianeme" (H-160).

In "The Parliament of Roses to Julia" (H-11), Herrick again exploits the possible relationship between Julia and the flowers:

> I Dreamt the Roses one time went
> To meet and sit in Parliament:
> The place for these, and for the rest
> Of flowers, was thy spotlesse breast:
> Over the which a State was drawne
> Of Tiffanie, or Cob-web Lawne;
> Then in that *Parly*, all those powers
> Voted the Rose; the Queen of flowers.
> But so, as that her self should be
> The maide of Honour unto thee.

6. Cf. Whitaker, "Herrick and the Fruits of the Garden," p. 21. The "beames" in this reading are material polyps of coral, not emitted rays.

The poem is held together by the links drawn between the human and the natural, and by the subordinate imagery of government: parliament, state (here a pun on canopy), powers, queen, maid of honor. The point of this little ceremony is that the election of a queen of flowers is but to choose a maid for Julia, the true "Queen of flowers." The uniqueness of the lyric is not in what is said, but in how it is said. The careful recounting of the flowers' action, the gradual heightening of the significance of that action, and the suddenly inverted "placing" of that significance in the larger perspective of the final two lines all aid the effectiveness of the compliment.

"Upon Roses" (H-78) also illustrates Herrick's ability to revitalize what might normally be fairly stock floral imagery:

> UNder a Lawne, then skyes more cleare,
> Some ruffled Roses nestling were:
> And snugging there, they seem'd to lye
> As in a flowrie Nunnery:
> They blush'd, and look'd more fresh then flowers
> Quickned of late by Pearly showers;
> And all, because they were possest
> But of the heat of *Julia's* breast:
> Which as a warme, and moistned spring,
> Gave them their ever flourishing.

The roses, in their "flowrie Nunnery," are "more fresh then flowers" —they are rendered immutable because they exist in a realm of "ever flourishing." The correspondence here is so deftly established that it is possible to miss the actual tenor of the metaphor—the nipples of Julia's breasts. The delicacy of the expression, the precise choice of individual words (such as "ruffled" roses), the detailed but concise description, the controlled inversion of the focus (which still carries on but goes further than the correspondence already established)—all help to make the poem a perfect example of the wit and achievement of the verse-compliment.

The kinds of statements made in these three poems are typical of the compliments throughout the *Hesperides*, not only with reference to

Julia, but to all of the poet's fifteen mistresses, and not only with roses, but with violets, lilies, cherries, and so forth. Inevitably the point of the compliment is that the natural object in some way serves the mistress, or that the mistress contains within her all the excellences of the object. This theme is perhaps a limited extension of a presupposition involving the Chain of Being: each link on the chain incorporates, and then goes beyond, each preceding link. Frequently, though, Herrick turns correspondence into contrast by arguing that the natural object is subject to the changing seasons, to the cyclic pattern of birth-death-rebirth, whereas Julia is not. Ultimately, of course, this kind of compliment breaks down, for Julia is tied just as securely to the natural cycle. Although this fact is not often faced in the compliments themselves, it is sometimes hinted, as perhaps in "Upon Julia's Recovery." And when that hint becomes overt, Herrick is forced to confront once again the major qualification he raises in the pastorals.

A second type of verse-compliment makes use of micro-macrocosmic correspondences. The clearest example is "The Eye" (H-133), in which the speaker asks a painter to draw him a heaven, complete with "straight, and oblique lines," "Motions, Lations, and the Signes," "a Chariot, and a Sun," "a Zodiac," "Zones, and Tropicks," "all the Seasons of the Yeare," "Cloudes to poure downe raine," and all the other "natural" features of the sky. When the artist has done this, says the speaker, he will have re-created Corinna's eye. "Upon her Eyes" (H-524) is a better poem on the same subject:

> CLeere are her eyes,
> Like purest Skies.
> Discovering from thence
> A Babie there
> That turns each Sphere,
> Like an Intelligence.

The brevity of the statement is its clearest asset: a two-line simile springs a four-line metaphor. The mistress's pupil ("Babie") is analogous to one of the angels controlling the heavenly spheres. By making its point and ending, the rhetorical understatement is effective in evoking an entire realm of correspondences through a single, well-chosen parallel.

Although these two types of complimentary lyrics are perfectly conventional in Cavalier poetry, and although Herrick does revitalize them considerably, he also goes beyond them to others which are less typical. He often describes, for instance, slight situations involving his mistresses or sometimes even himself: Julia falling, Corinna gathering flowers, his tying Anthea's shoe, and so forth. These poems are still verse-compliments, but depend less on stock situations and analogies than on actual, human dramas in which the mistress becomes not merely the focal point of a compliment, but a live person. The argument that Herrick's mistresses are not real because he never describes them or because he does not seem to have any feeling for them as people simply will not hold.[7] True, we do not know what Julia looks like, and she could easily be interchanged with Corinna; but she is a real woman—we know how she acts, how she dresses, how her robes flow, and how the speaker of Herrick's lyrics responds to her. Most of these mistresses are seen in some kind of precise action, a rare occurrence in other Cavalier verse.

"Upon Julia's Fall" (H-27) is a good example of this type of compliment:

> *J U*lia was carelesse, and withall,
> She rather took, then got a fall:
> The wanton *Ambler* chanc'd to see
> Part of her leggs sinceritie:
> And ravish'd thus, It came to passe,
> The Nagge (like to the *Prophets Asse*)
> Began to speak, and would have been
> A telling what rare sights h'ad seen:
> And had told all; but did refraine,*
> Because his Tongue was ty'd againe.

[*from Latin *refrenare*, to bridle back—Patrick's note]

7. See Delattre, *Robert Herrick*, pp. 213–14; Gosse, *Seventeenth Century Studies*, p. 133; Moorman, *Robert Herrick*, pp. 214, 236.

The tongue-tied nag is but a final closural delight here. The poem is an ingenious working out of a dramatic situation and we respond to the action itself, although much of the effect of that action depends upon the use of the latinate "sinceritie." What other courtly mistress falls? This perfectly ungenteel act is transformed by Herrick into an exquisite compliment. Even the subtle joke on Julia in the second line serves to make more vivid the human situation. And the ambler, of course, might refer to a man as well as a horse. This too serves to increase the drama of the action and to make credible the image of Julia herself. Here is a real, live woman, not one of those airy figures of most Cavalier poems. The same type of compliment can be found in "The shooe tying" (H-33) and "Upon Julia's washing her self in the river" (H-939).

"Another upon her weeping" (H-743) illustrates Herrick's ability to compress these poems of action into concise, emblematic statements:

> SHe by the River sate, and sitting there,
> She wept, and made it deeper by a teare.

The point depends upon a contrast: the mistress' tear is but one minute drop of water when compared to the river, yet the *action* of the poem, her weeping, makes that single tear far more significant than all the water. "Deeper" is thus both ironic and serious, but the implications of "deeper meaning" overshadow the irony and control the tone of the poem. Herrick effects the entire emotional tenor of the couplet by one carefully chosen word.

Another effective device Herrick uses in his compliments is to concentrate on objects of the mistress rather than the mistress herself. Into this class falls one of his most famous compliments, "Upon Julia's Clothes (H-779)." "Julia's Petticoat" (H-175) is constructed on an image similar to that in the more familiar poem, but carries it further:

> THy Azure Robe, I did behold,
> As ayrie as the leaves of gold;
> Which erring here, and wandring there,
> Pleas'd with transgression ev'ry where:

Sometimes 'two'd pant, and sigh, and heave,
As if to stir it scarce had leave:
But having got it; thereupon,
'Two'd make a brave expansion.
And pounc't with Stars, it shew'd to me
Like a *Celestiall Canopie.*
Sometimes 'two'd blaze, and then abate,
Like to a flame growne moderate:
Sometimes away 'two'd wildly fling;
Then to thy thighs so closely cling,
That some conceit did melt me downe,
As Lovers fall into a swoone:
And all confus'd, I there did lie
Drown'd in Delights; but co'd not die.
That Leading Cloud, I follow'd still,
Hoping t'ave seene of it my fill;
But ah! I co'd not: sho'd it move
To Life Eternal, I co'd love.

The poem begins with a pun: the robe is "ayrie" by virtue of its color and by virtue of its actions. The pun serves as a structural device, for each of these relationships between the robe or petticoat and the sky is developed in the next twenty lines: lines 3–8 and 11–18 discuss the "ayrie-ness" of the robe's actions; lines 9–10 and 19–22, the "ayrie-ness" of its color.

The first description of the robe is similar to the aesthetic principle set forth in "Delight in Disorder" (H-83):

> A Sweet disorder in the dresse
> Kindles in cloathes a wantonnesse.
>
> (ll. 1–2)

The "transgression" of line 4 is the flowing of the robe: because it does not remain stationary, it seems to break decorum. Likewise, the "wantonnesse" is here specifically human in nature and functions to personify further the petticoat itself. It pants, sighs, heaves, desires to be free from restrictions, and takes full advantage of that freedom when it is offered. Herrick delights in this assigning of human emotions to the object being described, presumably because it allows him to give the object surrounding the mistress emotions or actions which, if ascribed directly to Julia herself, would violate decorum and propriety.[8] The poem does not go so far as to suggest that Julia herself "transgresses" in any way, but it is clear that the character of the petticoat excites the beholder in terms of her. If this were not the case, lines 17–18, including the obvious pun on the word "die," would lose much of their coy effect. The "*Celestiall Canopie*" of line 10 gives way, in the final four lines, to an image of the moving, wispy, everchanging cloud-petticoat which leads the speaker on in the hope of "seeing his fill," just as the Israelites were led by a "pillar of cloud" by day. By ceremonially re-creating the total vision of Julia in terms of this single object, Herrick invites the reader to respond to her in the same way he does—to see, that is, how beguiling and bewitching she and her petticoat can be.

"Her Bed" (H-348) also depends upon this method of praising the mistress by focusing on one of her objects:

> SEe'st thou that Cloud as silver cleare,
> Plump, soft, & swelling every where?
> Tis *Julia's* Bed, and she sleeps there.

The analogy is one the poet frequently uses: Julia's bed is like a cloud; in turn, the characteristics of that cloud are those of Julia herself. The real success of the poem, however, lies in the last four words, "and she sleeps there." The reader is taken abruptly from the realm of fanciful analogy to one of human actuality. The effectiveness of the poem depends, as in "Upon her Eyes," on the poet's wit combined with his sense of timing. The reader is led to anticipate in line three an extension of the opening analogy, perhaps even a suggestive extension;

8. Cf. the judgment by H. M. Richmond that Herrick's poems "are often illuminating and picturesque when seen as methods of ingenious sublimation or transference of emotions which might otherwise threaten his emotional stability" (*The School of Love* [Princeton, 1964], p. 146).

instead he gets a surprisingly literal statement which points even more suggestively than the expected metaphor.

All of these verse-compliments are ceremonial. They celebrate the significance of either the mistress or the objects surrounding her (though even here it is really the mistress herself who is being celebrated). In such poems as "The Parliament of Roses," the ceremonial provides a miniature rite at which the mistress reigns as the supreme beauty while devotees come to worship her. In other poems, the elevating or exalting of the mistress to a greater level of importance than she would normally have, whether by means of correspondence, analogy, or ritualistic actions she either does or inspires, also heightens the significance of the lover's response to her. These poems illustrate that the act of loving necessarily involves certain precise functions on the part of the courtly lover, one of which is "singing" the praises of the mistress. That "singing" is given ritualistic nature by the manner in which it is conducted. The rite of complimenting, in other words, is a formal and religious act of celebration in which the lover, by definition, must participate. The *poetic* ceremonial is thus a vehicle providing form and substance, as well as meaning, to the love-situation.

The third lyric-type spoken by Herrick's Cavalier wit is the protestation. It occurs in numerous forms, but the most common are a speaker protesting against the trials and misfortunes love has put him through ("The Frozen Heart" [H-13]), a protestation to the mistress concerning the depths of his love ("To Anthea, who may command him any thing" [H-267]), a protesting of his own independence ("Love lightly pleased" [H-579]), and various treatments of the "impossibilities" motif ("His Protestation to Perilla" [H-154]).

The first of these forms is perhaps the one most commonly attributed to the Cavalier poets. In it the speaker describes, by the use of convenient and numerous apostrophes, how love has made him fry or freeze, laugh or weep, live or die—the same paradoxes of love seen in the lyrics of the Petrarchan love-situation. The only twist Herrick effects in the motif is his heavy concentration on what Cupid himself has done to the persona. He often sets up a game between the two in which the speaker, because he pities the erring boy for some misfortune into which he has fallen, is struck, pricked, or scorched in return for his kindness. Like the Petrarchan poems, these little dramas are fairly conventional, though not so trite as, for example, "The Frozen Heart."

The speaker's protestation of the depths of his love is also a conventional motif, but here Herrick works more distinct effects. The best example is "To Anthea, who may command him any thing":

BId me to live, and I will live
   Thy Protestant to be:
Or bid me love, and I will give
   A loving heart to thee.

A heart as soft, a heart as kind,
   A heart as sound and free,
As in the whole world thou canst find,
   That heart Ile give to thee.

Bid that heart stay, and it will stay,
   To honour thy Decree:
Or bid it languish quite away,
   And't shall doe so for thee.

Bid me to weep, and I will weep,
   While I have eyes to see:
And having none, yet I will keep
   A heart to weep for thee.

Bid me despaire, and Ile despaire,
   Under that *Cypresse* tree:
Or bid me die, and I will dare
   E'en Death, to die for thee.

Thou art my life, my love, my heart,
   The very eyes of me:
And hast command of every part,
   To live and die for thee.

The poem is unique by virtue of its tone: rhetorical amplification and hyperbole, so common to the protestation (as evidenced in the "impossibilities" motif, for instance), are here muted by the seeming naïveté of the speaker's bald declarations. The presence of hyperbole here cannot be denied, but the poem's emotional strength is effected more by the speaker's unpretentious and repetitive simplicity. In relation to other Cavalier "protestations," this one seems, despite its rhetoric, almost understated. And despite the opportunities the poem presents for parody of the motif, I see no evidence here that Herrick is treating the protestation sportively.

The poem begins with the witty play on the word "Protestant," which carries not only the connotation of one who solemnly declares his love by way of protestation, but also that of a religious devotee. In both cases, the speaker's whole reason for being alive is Anthea herself. The rest of the poem, after line 2, consists of a "protestation" fulfilling the vow made in this second line.

Lines 3–4 serve primarily as transitions preparing for stanzas two through four, all concerning the nature of the speaker's heart. It is soft, kind, "sound and free"—curiously enough, not "loving." That quality remains unstated and is proved only by the perfect willingness of the lover to do whatever his mistress might command. The most effective of the three stanzas is the final one (i.e., stz. 4), in which the speaker protests that should he lose his eyes weeping for Anthea, he would yet retain his heart to continue that weeping. The simple quatrain form yields a fine sense of controlled, but intense, emotion here. At times it has been assumed that the concise and controlled statements of Cavalier verse betray an underlying lack of emotional intensity, also assuming, it would appear, that such intensity naturally results in a more chaotic and uncontrolled verse form.[9] There can be

9. The rationale underlying this assumption is implicit in many of the critics who have written on Jonson and his followers. Edward Selig, for instance, asserts that Jonson's "artistic feeling, if not love, refined and ordered in a pattern of delicate strength, gives to his best lyrics a cool, assured poise, an idealism at once artificial and rational, hardly less compelling in its way than emotional intensity" (*The Flourishing Wreath* [New Haven, 1958], p. 41). Rufus Blanshard maintains that the artistry of the Cavalier lyric "is almost always a result not only of aesthetic but also of temperamental 'distance' " ("Carew and Jonson,"

no question of the force of the emotions in this poem, however, for a less powerful and sincere feeling could not allow ingenuous declaration to stand for and mirror the emotional state.

In stanza five the speaker is willing to dare even death for Anthea, should she bid him to do so. Though this bold claim is often heard from other poets of the age, there is here none of the more conventional rhetorical apostrophes usually accompanying such assertions: it is a blunt statement of willingness. Likewise, there is no real sense of the common pun on the word "die." The speaker "simply" claims that Anthea may command anything, bid him live or die, and he will eagerly obey.

The final stanza, in fact the whole poem, has distressed some readers because it seems too similar to the kind of statement constructed every day by thousands of young adolescents in their first full sense of love. It suggests too clearly, that is, the spirit of these early and somewhat feeble attempts to describe an emotion which is totally new and little known. But this is precisely the point. Surely one of the strengths of the poem, and of the final stanza in particular, is that although we know we are listening to a mature lover, the qualities of adolescent purity and wholeness of emotion are perfectly mirrored. Far from detracting from the poet's statement, such qualities are integral to it and immeasurably heighten it. We are taken back to a state or time in life when the emotion of love *is* the *all*, the life and death, of the lover, when affairs of the adult world and personal problems are irrelevant in the face of so overwhelming an emotion, when all that is of any concern is how to please the object of the affections. The feat of reinvoking the first adolescent response to love as a sign of the utter

Studies in Philology 52 [1955]: 209). And Matthew Black, after describing Herrick and Carew as "consummate stylists in construction, ordering of thought, choice and placing of words, and nicety of versification," as poets whose "every thought, every figure is carefully and finely wrought," goes on immediately to claim that both "are versatile without being either deep or passionate" (*Elizabethan and Seventeenth Century Lyrics* [Philadelphia, 1938], p. 384). Northrop Frye surely has the correct view on this matter: "The notion that convention shows a lack of feeling, and that a poet attains 'sincerity' (which usually means articulate emotion) by disregarding it, is opposed to all the facts of literary experience and history" (*Anatomy of Criticism* [1957; rprt. New York, 1966], p. 97).

purity of the maturer love and of the protestation itself is no small
achievement.[10] The poem succeeds by ceremonially capturing and
elevating a precise instant of human experience, and by "singing" the
ultimate value of that instant and that experience.

The third type of Cavalier protestation involves an assertion of the
speaker's utter independence, of his role as a courtier, detached yet
open to love from all sides. The tone of these protestations is totally
different from that of the former type, for here the emphasis is on a
calculated indifference to everything except the act of love. It is the
consummate tone of Donne's "The Indifferent" and displays more
openly one peculiar aspect of the Cavalier wit. Herrick's "Love lightly
pleased" (H-579) is an example of the type:

> LEt faire or foule my Mistresse be,
> Or low, or tall, she pleaseth me:
> Or let her walk, or stand, or sit,
> The posture hers, I'm pleas'd with it.
> Or let her tongue be still, or stir,
> Gracefull is ev'ry thing from her.
> Or let her Grant, or else Deny,
> *My Love will fit each Historie.*

The "faire or foule" of the first line suggests that this kind of lyric has
close affinities with the "praise-of-grotesque" genre, of which Shakespeare's Sonnet 130 is perhaps the prime example. But in this poem
the point is rather the depiction of the Cavalier himself: he is totally
indifferent to the kind of mistress he has, for he can adapt to any and
to all. Underlying protestations of this type is a basic unstated premise
that to the Cavalier all women are the same—an extension of the
common lady-versus-prostitute joke. Herrick puts the assumption in
more explicit terms in "In the darke none dainty" (H-586):

> NIght hides our thefts; all faults then pardon'd be:
> All are alike faire, when no spots we see.

10. Cf. Delattre's claim: Herrick speaks as a "grand enfant quelquefois,
qui aurait gardé la fraîcheur de ses impressions premières, et serait incapable
encore de les dissimuler" (*Robert Herrick*, p. 117).

Lais and *Lucrece*, in the night time are
Pleasing alike; alike both singular:
Jone, and my *Lady* have at that time one,
One and the selfe-same priz'd complexion.
Then please alike the Pewter and the Plate;
The chosen *Rubie*, and the *Reprobate*.

As in the former poem, the emphasis is less on the nature of women, although this idea is present, than on the Cavalier himself. It is again a protestation of his indifference to all save the act of love. Care must be taken, however, to note the tone of the poem, for the interest here is more a display of wit than anything else and poems of this type are attempts to be "pleasingly lascivious." This subtle but suggestive impropriety is often at the very base of the Cavalier wit (using "wit" in the modern sense of humor).[11]

The final type of protestation lyric involves the familiar "impossibilities" motif. Again Donne supplies the best known, though certainly not the first, analogue, "Goe, and catche a falling starre."[12] Herrick uses the convention in "His Protestation to Perilla" (H-154):

NOone-day and Midnight shall at once be seene:
Trees, at one time, shall be both sere and greene:
Fire and water shall together lye
In one-self-sweet-conspiring sympathie:
Summer and Winter shall at one time show
Ripe eares of corne, and up to th'eares in snow:
Seas shall be sandlesse; Fields devoid of grasse;
Shapelesse the world, (as when all *Chaos* was)
Before, my deare *Perilla*, I will be
False to my vow, or fall away from thee.

11. There is still no satisfactory study of humor in the *Hesperides*, despite the fact that Herrick is frequently as witty as Carew at his very best. Perhaps this lack of attention to the strictly humorous level of the poetry results from a tacit acknowledgment of the difficulties involved in trying to define the emotional stance of Herrick's speakers and his own relationship to them. Still, no study of the poet, including this one, can claim to be complete unless it treats his persistent wit.

12. For an earlier English version, see Lodge, "A Fancy" (*Rosalind*, 1590).

The poem is an elaborate hyperbolic statement at the opposite, or near-opposite, end of the rhetorical scale from "To Anthea." Constructed on the principle of natural antipathies which become impossibly united, it is little more than a rhetorical display of wit ("wit" here in the more common seventeenth-century meaning of bringing diverse things together in one statement). Not all of Herrick's "impossibilities" are so conventional, as "Impossibilities to his friend" (H-198) illustrates:

> MY faithful friend, if you can see
> The Fruit to grow upon the Tree:
> If you can see the colour come
> Into the blushing Peare, or Plum:
> If you can see the water grow
> To cakes of Ice, or flakes of Snow:
> If you can see, that drop of raine
> Lost in the wild sea, once againe:
> If you can see, how Dreams do creep
> Into the Brain by easie sleep:
> Then there is hope that you may see
> Her love me once, who now hates me.

The poem first deviates from convention by addressing not the mistress but a friend (although it is not the first to do this—see Donne's "Goe, and catch a falling starre"). This departure from tradition is not as important as the fact that the objects which the speaker describes are real, not "impossibilities" at all. That is, attention is directed here not at a product, as is common in such poems, but at a process. The color of a pear or plum can certainly be seen (unlike noon and midnight *at once*), but it is not possible to see the fruit actually coloring. Herrick presents this impossibility of transparent insight in order to prepare for the play of wit at the end of the poem. At first glance, the "see" of line 11 seems to mean the conventional "find" rather than the ability to perceive changes occurring. And surely this reading is valid on one level: the condition of the mistress' loving the speaker is an impossible one. But he could also be implying that this state is, or will be, an actual one and that his friend will not be able to "see" the process by which this change in the mistress comes about. In this sense, the connotation of "see" is the same as in the rest of the poem, as is the relationship between the see-er and the state of the object. In either case, the poem is a clear demonstration of Herrick's ability to infuse new life into a conventional genre.

The fourth lyric type used by the Cavalier persona is the dialectical or argumentative debate. These poems usually present dramatic situations in which the speaker argues some point with the mistress, often the necessity of consummating their affair immediately. The emphasis in the poems, however, is less on that consummation, or whatever the point being argued, than on the argument itself. The most typical of Herrick's debate poems is "To his Mistresse objecting to him neither Toying or Talking" (H-38):

> YOu say I love not, 'cause I doe not play
> Still with your curles, and kisse the time away.
> You blame me too, because I cann't devise
> Some sport, to please those Babies in your eyes:
> By *Loves Religion*, I must here confesse it,
> The most I love, when I the least expresse it.
> *Small griefs find tongues*: Full Casques are ever found
> To give (if any, yet) but little sound.
> *Deep waters noyse-lesse are*; And this we know,
> *That chiding streams betray small depth below.*
> So when Love speechlesse is, she doth expresse
> A depth in love, and that depth, bottomlesse.
> Now since my love is tongue-lesse, know me such,
> Who speak but little, 'cause I love so much.

The poem's argument by analogy is similar to the witty reasoning we find in Donne or Carew,[13] although it is distinct from the arguments of the "metaphysical school" because of the absence of any polarized

---

13. Although both poets provide numerous examples of this kind of argument, the closest analogue to Herrick's poem is Raleigh's "The Secret Love" (quoted in Norman Ault's *Elizabethan Lyrics* [New York, 1949], pp. 284–85).

tension between the vehicles and the tenors of the different analogies.
Instead of exploiting the literally incompatible figures of the analogies
in order to heighten the significance of the submerged similarities, as
Donne often does, Herrick accepts his analogies at face value; they
are but minor premises in the syllogistic argument and need not be
extended beyond mere aphoristic form.[14]

The first four lines of the poem present the dramatic situation of
the mistress complaining about the speaker's lack of expression, either
"Toying or Talking." The remainder of the poem is his answer to
the charge. He begins, in line 5, by referring to the courtly code involved. "By *Loves Religion*" is neither a vague allusion nor a mean-
ingless oath; it evokes an entire ethos, a ritual of wooing and of being
wooed, the courtly "game" of love. The use of the word "religion" is,
of course, a polemic ruse defining the speaker as a devotee and elevating
or sanctifying the argument which he presents. The mistress must
accept at least the basic premise of this argument, for by referring to
"*Loves Religion*" the speaker deliberately casts that premise in the
guise of a confession: "I must here confesse it." The mistress becomes
a confessor-priestess rather than a complainer and has no choice at this
point but to accept the protestation that the more he loves the less he
expresses it.

The next four lines of the poem (ll. 7–10) present a series of three
analogies to support the premise given in line 6: small griefs find
quickest expression, full casks give less sound than empty ones, and
deep waters make less noise than shallow ones. Given these proverbial,
and hence unquestionable, analogies, the speaker draws the logical
conclusion, first in the form of a general postulate, then in terms of his
own situation: love is deepest when it is most speechless and he as a
lover speaks little because he loves so much. The lover has successfully
defended himself against the mistress's charge.

There is an additional argumentative twist in the poem, however,
which places the mistress herself in the wrong; instead of defense, the

14. Cf. Selig's discussion of "polarized tensions" in Donne and Carew in *The
Flourishing Wreath*, p. 102; and Rufus Blanshard's distinction between Metaphysical and Cavalier "conceits" in "Carew and Jonson," pp. 196ff.

debate turns offensive. "Small griefs find tongues." Though the proverb functions mainly in terms of the analogical development, it also
serves as a counter-protest against the mistress's opening complaint.
That complaint, suggests the lover, argues a certain "smallness" in
her love. The situation is suddenly reversed; now it is up to her to
respond with a protestation. Not content simply to excuse himself,
the lover demands a further excuse from her in return. "By *Loves
Religion*," the courtly game goes on.

The fact that these dialectical lyrics frequently deal with this kind
of courtly "game" relates them to the fifth Cavalier type in which
Herrick seems to delight, the game-lyric. The basic narrative focus
of these poems is on the playing of push-pin, cherry-pit, barley-break,
draw-gloves, and other literal court love-games. The lyrics are usually
sportive and often "pleasingly lascivious." They once more attempt
to depict or present one little ritual in *"Loves Religion."* "Cherry-pit"
(H-49) is representative:

> JUlia, and I did lately sit
> Playing for sport, at Cherry-pit:*
> She threw; I cast; and having thrown,
> I got the Pit, and she the Stone.

[*Cherry-pit: "game in which players try to throw cherry pits into a small hole
which, punningly, may also be called a pit"—Patrick's note.]

The metrical and verse form of this poem, as in most of the game-lyrics,
is that of the epigram. The first two lines present the situation or the
actual game and the final two provide the "turn" or reversal of
thought, or, in this case, the play of wit. As Patrick notes, the puns of
the final line depend upon a riddling folksong in which "a girl gives
her lover a cherry [still a slang usage] which has no stone [slang for
testicle] or pit, but ultimately she is herself heavy with consequences."

Most of the game-lyrics follow this format and conclude with this
type of word-play. They all begin, that is, by describing the game as
it is played, and conclude by applying either the actions of the game,
the positions of the players, or the technical terms of the game to a
courting situation, frequently a suggestive one. Such lyrics are another

example of Herrick's tendency to capture and elevate specific moments of larger experiences. These little games are made to stand for the whole ritual of courtly and Cavalier love. It *is* a sort of game, a contest in which the reward is a kiss or something more, and loss is a broken, burned, or at least scorched heart. Every act of wooing and love-making is formalized and ritualized.

"To Electra" (H-152) begins as a game-lyric, but ends as something slightly different:

> ILe come to thee in all those shapes
> As *Jove* did, when he made his rapes:
> Onely, Ile not appeare to thee,
> As he did once to *Semele*.
> Thunder and Lightning Ile lay by,
> To talk with thee familiarly.
> Which done, then quickly we'll undresse
> To one and th'others nakednesse.
> And ravisht, plunge into the bed,
> (Bodies and souls commingled)
> And kissing, so as none may heare,
> We'll weary all the Fables there.

Even the "game" of this lyric is unique. It is not the innocent sportive activity of the court, a public amusement turned into subtle and suggestive private action. Here the act of love-making is specific and open. The inclusion of the poem within this category rests simply on the treatment of that love-making. That is, the act itself is made a game by the speaker. There is no sense here of any attempt to make a serious statement about the nature of love, even though such a statement may, in fact, be made. It is simply the representation of a love-ritual, a rite of woo and be wooed, of "let's pretend we're the gods." If Herrick's game-lyrics do not present love in terms of an actual court game, they re-create the game setting and context by treating love as a minute ritual in which the lover and the mistress engage in order to actualize their relationship.

There are some other features of this particular poem which distinguish it from the simpler game-lyrics. It is constructed of a two-part movement: the first describes the central analogy; the second deflates that analogy. Thus, in lines 1–6, the speaker protests that he will visit the mistress in all the shapes of Jove save one. He presents the "matter" of his plea outright, for the emphasis of the first two lines falls clearly on "shapes" and "rapes." Carrying the analogy to its logical extreme, he assures her that he will lay his thunder and lightning aside to "talk" with her "familiarly." The carefully ordered progression of these six lines effectively mirrors the speaker's gradual assumption of the Jove-mask, and by line 6 he *is* Jove.

The second six lines invert the analogy and the identification which have been created. Though the outcome is implicit in the emphasis on undressing, the final reversal does not occur until the final two lines:

> And kissing, so as none may heare,
> We'll weary all the Fables there.

So it had been a "Fable" after all. The couple is brought forcefully back to the real world of love and seduction; they have progressed beyond the fictional and have re-entered the realm of the actual. The fanciful analogy of the opening movement is fractured. Furthermore, the vitality in the final half of the poem is noticeably absent in the relatively sterile description of the first half. There the speaker seems to be concerned primarily with the "game"; here he moves out of the game context into the literal event which the game mirrors. Once again Herrick is impressive in the effects he is able to achieve within a very limited and specialized form.

The next lyric-type of the Cavalier wit includes the parting verses. Herrick has three major poems of this kind: "His sailing from Julia" (H-35), "His parting from Mistresse Dorothy Keneday" (H-122), and "The parting Verse, or charge to his supposed Wife when he travelled" (H-465). The first two are, in the main, quite traditional. "His sailing" asks that Julia pray to the gods for his safe journey; "His parting" complains that Mistress Keneday did not show enough emotion at their farewells.

The third poem, "The parting Verse," is more interesting. Its first fifty-two lines charge the mistress to remain as faithful as Penelope and detail the kind of attraction she will have on men in his absence, as well as the various ways in which they will seek to win her favor. In general, this opening section bids the "wife" to "Stand for my comming, Sentinell." Lines 53–66 alter the tone of the poem by assuming that she may in fact fall prey to someone's lust. But, says the "husband," do not worry, for then you will become a martyr to love like Lucrece, Cyane, and Medullina. The coolness of the speaker's attitude in this section is in stark contrast to the passion of the surrounding sections. It is not easy to tell whether the "husband" is merely putting on a brave front or is perfectly serious, or whether Herrick is holding him up as a pathetic or a ridiculous lover. The final section of the poem (ll. 67–84) returns to the tone and attitude of the first and places ultimate emphasis on the "religious" nature of the charge which the speaker is giving the "wife" and on his hope to find in her "all faith of Woman-kind."

Although the middle section of the poem is ambiguous, the framing sections seem to require us to read the entire poem as serious, as expressing honest and troubled concern.[15] Presumably, Herrick is attempting to reproduce the agonies that a parting lover suffers in trying to communicate his fears to his "wife." Probably the most significant device by which Herrick accomplishes that reproduction is the emphasis on the speaker's alternating expressions of fear and trust: at one moment the mistress will be in grave danger because of the power of the forces against her and her own vulnerability as a woman, the next moment she will prevail against all odds simply because she is the most virtuous of women. The poem is effective not in terms of what it says about love or the nature of love in general, but about a lover placed in a specific situation and his response to that situation. It does not demand acceptance of, or agreement on the *value* of, the lover's statements, but it does ask us to recognize the validity of his feelings and the reality of his anxiety.

The final lyric-type in which the Cavalier wit expresses himself is

15. Moorman (*Robert Herrick*, p. 73) sees the poem as a "tissue of pure fantasy."

the advisory poem, of which there are two forms. In the first the
speaker warns the mistress that her present attitude toward him will
change when her situation changes. The most common theme is the
argument that the mistress should not be so proud, for age will humble
her. The second form begins as the speaker's answer to the mistress's
complaint and proceeds to warn that what she has been complaining
about may soon be argued against her. Again, the most common motif
is the complaint of the aging lover, which the speaker swiftly turns
around and re-applies to the mistress herself.

"To Dianeme" (H-160) is representative of the first advisory
type:

> SWeet, be not proud of those two eyes,
> Which Star-like sparkle in their skies:
> Nor be you proud, that you can see
> All hearts your captives; yours, yet free:
> Be you not proud of that rich haire,
> Which wantons with the Love-sick aire:
> When as that *Rubie*, which you weare,
> Sunk from the tip of your soft eare,
> Will last to be a precious Stone,
> When all your world of Beautie's gone.

Poems of this sort are, in at least one sense, parodic inversions of the
conventional verse-compliment. By repeating the stock analogies used
in the compliment, and by bringing to the surface the qualifications
of mutability inherent in some of those analogies, Herrick is able to
place the whole genre of verse-compliment in ironic perspective. The
Shakespearian image of the ruby "sunk" from the tip of the mistress's
ear could be used, in a compliment, to point up the mistress's beauty,
delicacy, or value; here it becomes an emblem of her susceptibility to
transience. In many ways, Herrick is facing here the same problem
noted at the end of the preceding chapter. After establishing the pastoral ethos and the pastoral vision, the rustic personae are forced to
confront the physical reality of mutability and death. In the courtly
and urban lyrics, the Cavalier persona cannot escape these facts either.

In spite of the grandeur and the importance which he shows are inherent to the courtly love-ritual, still "death mars the song."

In "To a Gentlewoman, objecting to him his gray haires" (H-
164A), Herrick again faces the problem:

> AM I despis'd, because you say,
> And I dare sweare, that I am gray?
> Know, Lady, you have but your day:
> And time will come when you shall weare
> Such frost and snow upon your haire:
> And when (though long it comes to passe)
> You question with your Looking-glasse;
> And in that sincere *Christall* seek,
> But find no Rose-bud in your cheek:
> Nor any bed to give the shew
> Where such a rare Carnation grew.
> Ah! then too late, close in your chamber keeping,
>   It will be told
>   That you are old;
> By those true teares y'are weeping.

The narrative situation here represents the second advisory form, but
the point of the poem is identical to that in the preceding one. The lady
will shortly discover that she is the same aging figure against which
she now complains. The facts of mutability and decay are inescapable.
And the speaker implies that the lady should be aware of this, aware
of the coming of age, death, and decay, or she is likely to assume an
invulnerability which will only increase the shock of recognition when
age finally does come.

The most explicit statement of the "advice" of these lyrics occurs
in "The Changes to Corinna" (H-232):

> BE not proud, but now encline
> Your soft eare to Discipline.
> You have changes in your life,
> Sometimes peace, and sometimes strife:
> You have ebbes of face and flowes,

As your health or comes, or goes;
You have hopes, and doubts, and feares
Numberlesse, as are your haires.
You have Pulses that doe beat
High, and passions lesse of heat.
You are young, but must be old,
And, to these, ye must be told,
Time, ere long, will come and plow
Loathed Furrowes in your brow:
And the dimnesse of your eye
Will no other thing imply,
    But you must die
    As well as I.

"Time" is the real culprit and death the very real end; there is no escape. Though the courtly ritual and the courtly code may take one for a few moments beyond the contemplation of this inevitable end, it is, nonetheless, inevitable. Here the sudden shortening of the final two lines serves to emphasize the austerity of death: the mistress will die and so will the speaker. Unlike many of the Cavalier poets, who soften the conclusions to this type of advisory lyric by turning back to the present love situation, Herrick squarely faces the problem he has raised. The abruptness of the final line here shows his speaker more personally concerned with death than the two preceding lyrics would have us assume. It is not simply that his mistress will die, but that her death signals his own as well. Like his pastoral counterpart, the Cavalier persona is unable to provide any lasting means of going beyond this death, or the processes of mutability and decay. "Putrefaction" is still the end "Of all that Nature doth entend."

All of the poems examined thus far are united by virtue of the Cavalier voice which speaks them. Furthermore, most of them are ceremonial in the sense that they isolate, order, elevate, and celebrate specific instants in the courtly love relationship. The ceremonial serves as a vehicle by which these instants are heightened in significance primarily because it provides a framework of ritualistic action. These little rites of wooing and love-making are the visible and formal manifestations of the value of the experience of love.[16] Complimenting a mistress *is* a significant act; so is parting from her. Each individual rite in the whole drama of courtly love is important and meaningful, providing the lover with a means of expressing his feelings and the depth of his emotional commitment, as well as a public course for directing those feelings and that commitment.

The poetic ceremonial also provides a momentary refuge from the oppressive force of time by reproducing and hence making static or permanent the sanctity of the ritualistic moment. Ultimately, however, the attempt to escape time's cycle breaks down and the persona is forced to admit that *"Loves Religion"* will not last forever. This realization does not negate the importance of the ceremonies in which the courtly wit participates, but does qualify it. The ceremonial representations of the Cavalier persona leave the poet in the same position as those of the pastoral personae—confronting the reality of death. At this point no way out of the destructive process has been found; all the poet has done is to realize that neither the pastoral nor the courtly approach will be successful in the end.

ii. THE FUNCTIONARY VOICE

The second guise of the courtly persona is the functionary. His primary purpose is dedicatory and he "sings" the importance of either public figures, especially the King and his own personal patrons, or public events, such as the marriages of court celebrities. In both cases his lyrics are ceremonial and they invite the reader to join in the celebration of the specific person to whom they are addressed or the specific action they depict. In comparison with those courtly poems discussed in the preceding section, these are even more public. In fact, their very public nature imposes certain limitations on the poet and these poems are, consequently, the most traditional lyrics of his volume. They appeal, or seek to appeal, to a limited courtly audience with fairly stock expectations.

16. Cf. Deming, "The Classical Ceremonial," p. 60.

The lyric forms used by the courtly functionary are three: lyrics of a wholly public character praising the King, the Queen, or some other member of the royal family; poems of a more social character praising a court patron and usually seeking some form of praise in return; and lyrics again of a wholly public nature praising court events.[17] Because each form is perfectly conventional, a single example of each will suffice.

Poems in praise of the royal family are virtually required of the Cavalier poet, and Robert Herrick is no exception. His lyrics of this kind range from that dedicating the *Hesperides* to Prince Charles, through those blessing the young prince, through public lamentations over the King's political difficulties and separation from his Queen, to those celebrating different victories of the King over the Parliamentarian forces. This group of poems, although relatively small in number, again indicates the danger of assuming Herrick either refuses or is unable to see what is happening around him. Far from being unaware of the great political upheaval taking place, Herrick voices his horror of the events and proves himself a firm and loyal supporter of the King. "TO THE KING, Upon his comming with his Army into the West" (H-77) is a convenient example of his royalist position:

> WElcome, most welcome to our Vowes and us,
> Most great, and universall *Genius*!
> The Drooping West, which hitherto has stood
> As one, in long-lamented-widow-hood;
> Looks like a Bride now, or a bed of flowers,
> Newly refresh't, both by the Sun, and showers.
> War, which before was horrid, now appears
> Lovely in you, brave Prince of Cavaliers!
> A deale of courage in each bosome springs
> By your accesse; (*O you the best of Kings!*)
> Ride on with all white *Omens*; so, that where
> Your Standard's up, we fix a Conquest there.

17. The implicit distinction here between "public" and "social" is based upon Miner's discussion of the terms in *The Cavalier Mode*, pp. 3–42.

Like all dedicatory lyrics, this one is a public celebration. The major images of lines 2–6 are fairly common in Herrick's functionary poems: the west country is "Drooping" in the same way a flower wilts from lack of sun or rain. The King, as the sun (Herrick first uses this conventional image in the dedicatory poem to Prince Charles) and as a newly-refreshing shower, once more revives the drooping land. Juxtaposed with the natural image is a human one which reverses the correspondence of the former. Just as the King is seen as a natural object in order to define his relationship with the country, the west itself is personified in order to relate it to the King—it is a bride long awaiting the arrival of the bridegroom. The point of the juxtaposition is that the human and natural realms are united in the figure of the King, the divinely-sanctioned lord of both.

The poem then turns to demonstrating that the King influences the people of the west as he has influenced the country itself. He becomes, in lines 9–12, more than a "Prince of Cavaliers"; he is almost a god-figure, overflowing with and inspiring love in those who behold him—although here "courage" is substituted for the more traditional virtue of love because the time is obviously one of militancy. This image is related to the refreshing sun in the first half of the poem: as the sun brings warmth and life to the flowers, the King brings courage and vitality to the people; each, moreover, accomplishes this feat simply by being present.

Herrick's use of conventional imagery in the poem is calculated to arouse a response of celebration in the reader. He presents a static instant of experience in which all creation is momentarily unified in the office and the figure of the king and in the act of praising that king. The poem seeks neither agreement with nor even consideration of the issues involved in the political strife; it neither persuades parliamentarians nor stirs royalists to action. Its entire purpose is simply to evoke an intuitive affirmative response of joy and praise toward this particular personage in this particular moment.

Herrick's poems addressing his patrons are slightly more personal than the public eulogies, and they are more complex because they make several appeals simultaneously. They do present a public celebration

of the individual to whom they are directed, but they also suggest a
more social level of friendship and camaraderie, and they frequently
demand a response from that individual—usually a sign of some sort
that the poetry to which the poem alludes and for which he is asked
to serve as patron has been received with favor. "To Joseph Lord
Bishop of Exeter" (H-168) is a good example of this kind of
dedication:

> WHom sho'd I feare to write to, if I can
> Stand before you, my learn'd *Diocesan*?
> And never shew blood-guiltinesse, or feare
> To see my Lines *Excathedrated* here.
> Since none so good are, but you may condemne;
> Or here so bad, but you may pardon them.
> If then, (my Lord) to sanctifie my Muse
> One onely Poem out of all you'l chuse;
> And mark it for a Rapture nobly writ,
> 'Tis Good Confirm'd; for you have Bishop't it.

Herrick makes his appeal to Hall in the latter's own ecclesiastical language and uses that language to elevate and "sanctifie" both the patron
and the poem. The ecclesiastical terms transform what would otherwise be a fairly simple encomium into a quasi-ritualistic celebration in
which the reader and the patron are asked to participate.

It may seem curious that I have selected an example of the functionary persona's work which omits any reference to the most conspicuous characteristic of Herrick's lyrics to his patrons—his promise of
poetic immortality to those whom he has crowned with a poem. There
is nothing unique in this promise, for most of the poets of the age make
it at one time or another, to one person or another. However, given
the deep concern each of Herrick's personae shows over the problem
of mutability and the transience of all earthly things, given the quantity
and the various forms of this particular promise throughout the *Hesperides*, and given the insistence and the seriousness with which the
promise is made, it is obvious that Herrick is far from conventional
or typical in his use of it. The promise of poetic immortality takes on

a special ceremonial form and function in Herrick's verse and for that reason discussion of the immortality lyrics must be postponed until the final chapter. All that is necessary at this point is to emphasize that the present treatment of the dedicatory persona and the forms which he uses are carefully and deliberately limited.

The final lyric-type in which the dedicatory persona works is the celebration of specific courtly events, most notably court marriages. Again his purpose is to celebrate both the event and the participants, and again his poems must be seen as primarily ceremonial. Because of the totally public nature of the marriage event, and because of the strong line of tradition into which these poems fall, they are both more "artificial" and more literally ritualistic than the preceding functionary ones. In these poems there is no intrusion of the speaker at all. This is not to say there is no deliberate poetic consciousness at work here, but only that the speaker limits himself quite deliberately to the role of court singer and celebrator, without personal comment of any kind. He is as anonymous as the scop in an Old English song-lyric.

The generally conventional nature of Herrick's epithalamia does not require extensive analysis, though a definitive study of the epithalamic tradition is still needed and would have to include his work.[18] There is one feature of his poems, however, which does merit some attention. In both "A Nuptiall Song, or Epithalamie, on Sir Clipseby Crew and his Lady" (H-283) and "An Epithalamie to Sir Thomas Southwell and his Ladie" (H-149A), Herrick severely restricts the range of events depicted and concentrates on the culminating acts of the marriage day. His tendency to seize key ceremonial moments precludes the more expansive treatment of the entire day normally expected in an epithalamium.[19] This tendency is most obvious in the Southwell epithalamium, the first stanza of which clarifies Herrick's restricted scope:

18. The most comprehensive treatment of the genre is Virginia Tufte's *The Poetry of Marriage* (Los Angeles, 1970).

19. On the general structure of a conventional epithalamium and the chronology of the events depicted, see Thomas Greene, "Spenser and the Epithalamic Tradition," *Classical Journal* 9 (1957): 215–19; and Charles Osgood, "Epithalamion and Prothalamion: 'and theyr Eccho Ring'," *Modern Language Notes* 76 (1961): 205–08.

NOw now's the time; so oft by truth
Promis'd sho'd come to crown your youth.
 Then Faire ones, doe not wrong
 Your joyes, by staying long:
 Or let Love's fire goe out,
 By lingring thus in doubt:
 But learn, that Time once lost,
 Is ne'r redeem'd by cost.
Then away; come, *Hymen* guide
To the bed, the bashfull Bride.

Not only is the poem limited to the single act of bedding the bride,[20] but Herrick begins with that sense of urgency usually reserved for the concluding movement of an epithalamium. Throughout the remainder of the poem Herrick repeats the *carpe diem* injunction given here. Certainly this injunction is conventional in the epithalamic tradition and is almost always the fitting conclusion to the marriage-day rites, but the urgency which forces Herrick's speaker to *begin* with it is not typical, nor is his belaboring of the point. Only one other instance of such an emphasis comes to mind—Donne's Lincoln's Inn epithalamium, in which the refrain, "To day put on perfection, and a womans name," serves to heighten the bride's need for complete fulfillment, which can be accomplished only by hastening the day's events to their legitimate end. In Herrick's poem, the poet seems to imply that more is at stake than simply the final act of the wedding day: the urgency of the appeal on this particular day is used almost as an emblem for the urgency on all other days as well. The insistence on the "taking" of time necessitates concentration on only the ultimate act of the wedding and heightens the significance of the whole marriage ritual. As stanza 13 of the poem suggests—

 And now, both Love and Time
 To their full height doe clime—

20. In classical rhetorical manuals, the bedding hymn was quite distinct from the marriage hymn. See Menander of Laodicea's *Peri Epideiktikon*, ed. Leonardi Spengel, *Rhetores Graeci*, III (Leipzig, 1856).

love and time both stand still for a brief, intensified instant to allow fulfillment of this phase of human experience. The restricted poetic ceremonial achieves the same end: it stops time for the duration of the poem to allow full participation in and recognition of the importance of this moment of ritualistic celebration. All of Herrick's epithalamia, whether conventional or individual, present a very stylized and "artificial" experience which is transformed by the ritualizing process into a formal and public ceremony in which both poet and reader participate.

Whether he speaks as a Cavalier wit or as a dedicating functionary, the courtly persona usually works within the ceremonial mode. His poems do not present as fully developed a philosophical system as the pastoral personae's do, but they still represent the same kind of ordering and heightening of experience and they make the same kind of appeal to the reader. Whether the individual poem "sings" the compliment of a mistress, protests the depths of a love, praises the king or a court wedding, it generally does so in a ritualized manner. Second, the courtly poems are as much concerned with stopping time as the pastorals, and they share with the pastorals an assumption about the value of the momentary ceremonial stasis. In both instances, Herrick suggests that the true importance of the courtly activities lies in his own and the reader's participation. The singing of a verse-compliment *is* a significant human experience, and a significant public ceremonial as well.

It has been said that Herrick's poems show clear affinities to the masque genre. Nowhere is this relationship more suggestive than in the verses of the courtly persona. His is a stylized, highly ordered, and, in some ways, simplified world. Events are important because they actualize the little ritualistic codes which make up the courtly existence. Each lyric in this vein is essentially the working out of one small part of the court experience, presenting little real anxiety, little worry or human difficulty, but rather the surface brilliance of an ultimately successful masque. Taken together, the whole body of courtly lyrics makes up a masque of this form of life. Each poem presents one more aspect of the particular urban sensibility and to enjoy the poem is to participate, perhaps even cultivate, that sensibility. The reader's participation is similar in this respect to the final dance of audience and actors in the court masque—it unites him in the celebratory rite of the courtly world.

Eventually, however, the courtly persona comes to realize that these rituals of behavior do not last, that time itself cannot be stopped for very long, that mutability and decay are literally but a moment away. It is the same qualification found in the pastoral poems. The use of each kind of persona may, in fact, be Herrick's attempt to experiment with different approaches to the problem of human transience. But although the fact of death is confronted in some of these poems, no answer has been found. The courtly ceremonies and the courtly ceremonial poetry are important by their very natures, but they do not seem capable, at this point, of providing any escape from or transcendence of the austere reality of death.

There is one guise of the courtly persona, however, yet to discuss— the strictly artistic one. Like his pastoral counterpart, this persona is more concerned with the presentation of a *poetic* ceremony than with anything else. That is, he is not concerned to present a verse-compliment, to display his wit, or to glorify a particular person; he is concerned with the presentation and the artistic amplification of a given moment of poetic celebration. Whatever the ostensible subject of the poem, the voice of this persona directs the reader's attention to the strictly literary act which the poem involves.

As with the artistic-pastoral persona, complete analysis of the artistic-courtly one must be delayed until the final chapter. However, the general nature of his lyrics can be suggested. The courtly artist usually works with two distinct forms of lyric, the Bacchic and the dedicatory. The first, an obvious extension of the *carpe diem* injunction, reproduces moments of typical "Tribe" frolic: the drinking of wine, the telling of jokes, the reciting of verse, the "taking" of time. The ceremonial of this form is an outward and active one; it seeks to involve the reader in the poetic ritual by intoxicating him with the "recreation" which poetry is capable of providing. The second form is a particular extension of the social lyric in which Herrick examines the possibility of poetic immortality. Here, perhaps more clearly and

more openly than in any of the poems discussed thus far, Herrick
tries to enlist the reader in the very act of poetic construction and
expression, in a unique kind of "singing." These poems explore the
"re-creative" power of verse.[21] In both forms the reader is asked to
view the poetic process through the eyes of the poet, to affirm the
effectiveness of his ceremonial mode, and to affirm in addition the
significance of that mode in achieving the kind of artistic transcendence for which all Herrick's personae have been seeking.

21. Joan Webber's provocative discussion of the two senses of "recreation"
informing Sir Thomas Browne's conception of art is equally applicable, I think,
to the poetry of Herrick. See *The Eloquent "I"* (Madison, 1968), pp. 149–83.

CHAPTER IV

THE REALISTIC
CEREMONIAL

No BODY of seventeenth-century poetry has been considered less deserving of that title than Robert Herrick's epigrams. They have been assailed as coarse, insensitive, base, vulgar, nasty—even, in the words of one anonymous critic, a "poetical pigsty."[1] Most of Herrick's early editors simply refused to publish them; later editors who did placed them in an appendix rather than in the *Hesperides* proper.[2] Fortunately, the two most recent editors, L. C. Martin and J. Max Patrick, reconstruct the volume as Herrick must have wanted it and restore the epigrams to their rightful place.

Just why these poems have created such a stir is easy enough to understand. The conventional view of Herrick—as a delicate miniaturist, a reveler in all sorts of delights, a painter of exquisite little portraits of Julia's clothes, a chronicler of quaint and joyous rustic festivals, a propounder of naïve and pious exhortations—fails miserably to square with the poet whose peculiar sensibilities are depicted in the epigrams, or at least in some of them. His early critics rejected that

1. See Delattre, *Robert Herrick*, pp. 148–49; Gosse, *Seventeenth Century Studies*, p. 139; and M. L. S. Lossing, "Herrick: His Epigrams and Lyrics," *University of Toronto Quarterly* 2 (1933): 247–48. The most fascinating bits of castigation come from Robert Southey: "We have lately seen the whole of Herrick's poems republished, a coarse-minded and beastly writer, whose dung-hill, when the few flowers that grew therein had been transplanted, ought never to have been disturbed" (*An Introductory Essay on the Lives and Works of our Uneducated Poets* [London, 1830], p. 83); and again: "Of all our poets this man appears to have had the coarsest mind. Without being intentionally obscene, he is thoroughly filthy, and has not the slightest sense of decency. . . . The reprint of 1825 has in the title-page a wreath with the motto 'perennis et fragrans.' A stinking cabbage-leaf would have been the more appropriate emblem" (*Southey's Common-place Book*, 4th Series [London, 1851], p. 303).

2. Such is the case in Alfred W. Pollard's *The Hesperides and the Noble Numbers*, 2 vols. (London, 1891).

side of the man most unappealing and kept only that congruent with their preconceptions.

There have, of course, been recent attempts to salvage this segment of Herrick's canon and to examine it in relation to the other poems. Richard Ross argues that the epigrams provide Herrick with a means of venting his rage at man's impropriety and incivility, that they represent "nature" devoid of "art," a literal and factual presentation of people as Herrick experienced them.[3] John Kimmey approaches the poems from roughly the same point of view: they are satiric exposés of human foibles.[4] My own quibble with these readings is that Herrick's basic intentions do not seem satiric at all. To be sure, the epigrams, at least the sportive ones,[5] do treat characters and incidents which are ostensibly more "realistic" than those in either the pastoral or the courtly lyrics, and they do focus generally on various instances of human excess. Nevertheless, the voice behind these poems is not a stern, moralistic judge, and his use of some of the weapons and stratagems of satire does not limit him to only satiric ends.

Although most Renaissance poets think of and use the epigram as a satiric genre, the form itself has proved almost as elusive to define as the lyric. The early Greek epigram, for instance, was

> a very short poem summing up *as though in a memorial inscription* what it is desired *to make permanently memorable* in a single action or situation. It must have the compression and conciseness of a real inscription, and in proportion to the smallness of its bulk must be highly finished, evenly balanced, simple and lucid. [My italics.][6]

3. Ross, " 'A Wilde Civilitie'," pp. 8–13, 19–21, 55–57, 87–88, 279–81. Cf. Rollin, *Robert Herrick*, pp. 38, 56, 78–79, 172.

4. Kimmey, "Robert Herrick's Satirical Epigrams," *English Studies* 51 (1970): 312–23.

5. It is important to remember that most discussions of Herrick's epigrams are concerned only with the sportive ones, yet, by my own rough count there are 310 sententious epigrams as opposed to only 177 sportive ones. In addition, the number of patently non-satiric epigrams is even greater if we count the laudatory ones, numbering about 76.

6. *Select Epigrams from the Greek Anthology*, ed. J. W. Mackail (London, 1890), p. 4.

Its prime functions were to commemorate, compliment, or dedicate; to express appreciation of beauty, nature, or art; or to expound an ethical view of life or religion. This definition is extremely close to that now associated with the lyric, save for the emphasis on the more "personal" or "subjective" quality of the latter. In actuality, though, the Renaissance epigrammatists who preceded Ben Jonson limited far more strictly the definition and the subject matter of their form. To the sixteenth-century poet, the epigram was simply "a short poem ending in a witty and ingenious turn of thought, to which the rest of the composition is intended to lead up."[7] This Roman rather than Greek emphasis on the "turn" dictated a two-part division for most epigrams: the first part, called the exposition, set forth the situation to be treated and functioned somewhat like the "composition of place" in a meditation; the second, called the conclusion or disclosure, effected the point, climaxed the reversal, or clinched the paradox.[8] The subject matter of the sixteenth-century epigram was also severely limited to two major areas: aphoristic statements of proverbial lore or satiric attacks on the foibles of mankind.

By the seventeenth century, however, Thomas Bastard and Ben Jonson had enlarged the range of subjects which could legitimately be treated in epigrammatic form and also sanctioned a greater freedom in the verse form itself.[9] Jonson returned the epigram to its Greek rather than Roman form by making it once more a vehicle for expressing a variety of tones and purposes: dedicatory, appreciative, commemorative, satiric, sportive, and so forth. It is important to remember that Herrick usually writes in the Greco-Jonsonian tradition.

7. *OED*, but compare Puttenham's discussion: ". . . therefore the poet deuised a prety fashioned poeme short and sweete . . . and called it *Epigramma*, in which euery mery conceited man might, without any long studie or tedious ambage, make his frend sport, and anger his foe, and giue a prettie nip, or shew a sharpe conceit in few verses" (G. Gregory Smith, *Elizabethan Critical Essays* [Oxford, 1904]: II, 56).

8. See T. K. Whipple, "Martial and the English Epigram from Sir Thomas Wyatt to Ben Jonson," *University of California Publications in Modern Philology* 10 (1920–25): 282; and Smith's discussion of this division in *Poetic Closure*, pp. 198–203.

9. See Moorman, *Robert Herrick*, p. 281; Whipple, "Martial and the English Epigram," p. 353; and Wesley Trimpi, *Ben Jonson's Poems: A Study of the Plain Style* (Stanford, 1962), pp. 60–76, 136–59, 167–90.

Although this history is common knowledge to those who have studied the development of the genre, its implications for Herrick's epigrams have not always been appreciated and some points need to be re-emphasized. First, the earliest epigrams are "memorial inscriptions," in many ways similar to the epitaph.[10] They commemorate or celebrate a particular person, situation, or view of experience. In most cases, such epigrams are ceremonial. Even when satiric, the epigram's "memorial inscription" attempts to capture and present, in the briefest possible form, the true "character" of the person or event being attacked. Likewise, the didactic epigram, though it might use a dialectical argument, still presents a finalized view of experience: it "discloses" precise truths in such a way as to evoke an instantaneous recognition and affirmation of those truths, and to make them memorable through the dogmatic concision of the expression.

The importance of these characteristics of the Greek epigram has been clarified by Barbara Herrnstein Smith. She begins by redefining the two parts of the epigrammatic form: instead of "exposition" and "conclusion," she argues that the verbal structure of an epigram is distinguished by a "thematic sequence which reaches a point of maximal instability and then turns to the business of completing itself."[11] But verbal structure or thematic sequence is only part of what we mean by "epigrammatic," as she goes on to explain:

> In speaking of an utterance, poem, or couplet as "epigrammatic," we refer not only to a kind of verbal structure but to an attitude toward experience, a kind of moral temper suggested by that very structure. The epigram seems to offer itself as a last word, an ultimately appropriate comment, a definitive statement.[12]

The latter feature of the epigram is seen as the all-important one. Referring to the origins of the form, she summarizes the point of the preceding paragraph:

10. Puttenham, in fact, asserts that "an Epitaph is but a kind of Epigram only applied to the report of the dead persons estate and degree" (*Elizabethan Critical Essays*, II, p. 58).

11. Smith, *Poetic Closure*, p. 199.

12. *Poetic Closure*, p. 207.

As an utterance, the epigram seems to be the last word on its subject. This quality can probably be referred to the origins of the form: engraved on tombs, statues, public buildings, or wherever an inscription was wanted to identify or characterize something both briefly and permanently, the epigram would stand, for all time, to all readers, as the ultimately appropriate statement thereupon.[13]

Therefore, to treat an experience in the epigrammatic form,

> is to strip it down, to cut away irrelevance, to eliminate the local, specific, and descriptive detail, to reduce it to and fix it in its most permanent and stable aspect, to sew it up for eternity. The epigrammatist does not have "Negative Capability"; he "irritably search[es] after fact and reason"; he is not "capable of being in uncertainty, Mysteries, doubts"; he is "incapable of remaining content with half knowledge."[14]

The intentions described here are identical with those of Herrick's realistic persona. He presents the elements of his existence *as they are* —factually, objectively, definitively.[15] "Realism" in this sense defines not simply the experience mirrored in the poem (Ross's "nature"), but the attitude of the poetic speaker toward that experience. He is certain that he is making a definitive assertion about some aspect of his existence and his statements always have Ms. Smith's sense of finality about them. He is concerned, in other words, with memorializing his statements, whether they be of individual characters or general truths, with "fixing" them in their "most permanent and stable" aspect (stasis). Furthermore, the epigrammatic speaker invites his readers to affirm the validity and the truth of his assertion by celebrating not only its ultimate significance but its *right* to epigrammatic treatment, to finalized and memorialized form. The ceremony of realism, then, can be defined as the rite of definitive pronouncement: as the courtly

13. *Poetic Closure*, p. 196.
14. *Poetic Closure*, p. 208.
15. Rollin also concludes that the persona of the epigrams is "one who simply purports to show 'the way things are' " (*Robert Herrick*, p. 38).

poems turn private acts into public rituals, so the rite of definitive pronouncement transforms private thoughts into universally accepted truths.

The difficulty with such a definition, of course, is that on one level the epigrams are not ceremonial at all, at least not in the same way that the pastoral and courtly lyrics are. In those poems at least one meaning of "ceremonial" referred to a rite which the lyric either imitated or constructed. Here the "rite" is the speaker's treatment of his experience, not a separate act which he reports or repeats. The matter is complicated when we see that the speakers in these poems do not simply present what is real, but seem literally to revel in actuality. Herrick seems, in other words, to turn deliberately from the uncertainties and the qualifications raised by the courtly and pastoral personae to a more conclusive, more definitive, portrait of existence. If he cannot escape the realities of the human condition, one alternative is to give in completely to them, to accept them and celebrate them for what they are. The tone of all Herrick's ceremonial poems is dogmatic, of course, but while the dogmatism of the pastoral and courtly poems affirms the significance of the approaches to life they record, it unwittingly insists as well on the fact of mutability or impermanence undermining those approaches. In the epigram, however, the dogmatism admits no qualifying notes and yields for that reason a more definitive statement. The genre represents for the poet the weight of surety which anchors him fast amid uncertainties. His ceremonial, therefore, is his *own* ritual of deliberately constructing a celebration of reality on its terms. By affirming the exactness and the preciseness of the poet's statement, the reader actively joins him in the ritual memorializing of that specific aspect of experience.

Like most Renaissance collections of epigrams, Herrick's falls into two distinct groups, each characterized by its own limited persona. The first group is the work of an epigrammatic wit and the poems he speaks are either sportive or vulgar. The persona here is defined by a clear detachment from and superiority to his subject, as well as by a sense of irony in his treatment of that subject. In the sportive epigrams he is further identifiable as a parodist of sorts: his poems are not so much satiric attacks on the foibles of man as simply a playing with epigrammatic conventions. They are strictly "witty." In the vulgar epigrams the wit is overshadowed by a giving in to and perhaps an actual delight in the grotesque; although the wit is still present, its function is considerably qualified by the nature of the presentation and the material treated. Both groups are poetic exercises, for the ingenuity of the statement is the cardinal reason for the poem's existence. Nonetheless, both groups present static moments of experience or portraits of individuals which are given a heightened significance, as well as definitiveness and permanence, by the form in which they are cast.

Herrick's second body of epigrams contains the gnomic or sententious ones. Here wit gives way to explicit didacticism and these poems are distinctly hortatory. The persona, like the former, is characterized by detachment, superiority, and, to a lesser degree, a sense of irony. Unlike the witty persona, who plays with conventions and traditions, the gnomic voice plays with ideas and seeks to present the elemental truths of human experience. He always makes definitive pronouncements whose acceptance is guaranteed by the very nature of the epigrammatic form. The reduction of all concepts to proverbial limit renders them unquestionable and undebatable. The reader's response to such epigrams involves what can be termed a moment of shared awareness: his affirmation of the truth of the poet's pronouncement unites him with the artist for the duration of the poem. The celebration of what the epigram says, in other words, is a participation in the ceremony of definitive statement, or the realistic ceremonial. The irony of these epigrams is that their very dogmatism causes problems for the poet, because his treatment of particular "truths" proves universal applications which he is himself unwilling to admit.

i. THE SPORTIVE VOICE

Herrick's witty epigrams focus generally on comic situations and characters, and word-games. "Upon Batt" (H-184) is typical of the form and the persona:

> *BAtt* he gets children, not for love to reare 'em;
> But out of hope his wife might die to beare 'em.

In most of these poems Herrick tries to "real-ize" a specific individual by presenting a single defining act or feature. The point is to make the "act" comic or satiric, depending upon the detachment of the speaker, though Herrick is rarely satiric and nearly all of these epigrams are simply comic. In "Upon Batt," the opening line presents the situation to be exploited; the second effects the comic reversal. Structurally, the phrase "not for love to reare 'em" of line 1 may give away too soon the "turn" of the final line. In a strict sense, any division of the poem into "exposition" and "disclosure" would necessitate a break after "children" in line one. The poem thus breaks a cardinal structural rule for all epigrams: effect the point, or turn, in the briefest possible space, even in the final word itself. Despite his general mastery of poetic structures, Herrick is not as effective in this kind of concise inversion as he might be. It is clear, though, that the speaker of the poem is considerably removed from his subject. He is so superior to Batt, in fact, that it would distort the tone to claim the work is written out of any "moral indignation" over Batt's character or conduct. Batt functions quite simply as a device allowing the speaker to construct a joke, and the poem is a display of wit rather than the "disclosure" of some human foible.

Herrick's use of the final word of the epigram as the "disclosure" occurs in "Upon Judith" (H-356):

> *JUdith* has cast her old-skin, and got new;
> And walks fresh varnisht to the publick view.
> Foule *Judith* was; and foule she will be known,
> For all this fair *Transfiguration.*

Again the epigram divides into two parts, corresponding to the two couplets (which is the most typical verse form in these sportive poems). The first two lines present the imitated "action"; the second two draw the conclusion about that action. All of the emphasis, however, is centered upon the final word, "*Transfiguration.*" The image of the "Foule" mistress as "fresh varnisht" is a familiar one in Renaissance poetry, especially in Jonson's satires on courtly affectation.[16] But the coupling of this image with the religious term yields a startling irony. The incongruity reduces Judith's act to the level of the ridiculous. It is important to understand, however, that the ridicule is not a satiric attack but a witty joke. Satire depends upon our seeing that the speaker, despite his affected detachment, feels sincerely threatened by the subject under attack. In this poem, the speaker is totally detached; there is no threat, no sense of the situation impinging upon him in any way. The efficient cause of the piece is to effect the point—the juxtaposition of the foul, varnished Judith and the mystical concept of transfiguration.

The same kind of incongruous analogy is found in "Upon Zelot" (H-666):

> IS *Zelot* pure? he is: ye see he weares
> The signe of *Circumcision* in his eares.

The juxtaposition of the criminal implications (cropping the ears is a punishment for theft or inability to pay a debt) and religious devotion, and the bringing of the two together by the pun on circumcision, results in an ironic analogy. As in the preceding poem, the religious term functions primarily to reduce and ridicule the individual; it also, of course, suggests his deviation from the "religious" moral norm, but not necessarily to satirize him as much as to effect the joke.

In "Upon Blinks" (H-834) Herrick exploits the possibilities of epigrammatic language:

> *TOm Blinks* his Nose is full of wheales, and these
> *Tom* calls not pimples, but *Pimpleides*:
> Sometimes (in mirth) he sayes each whelk's a sparke
> (When drunke with Beere) to light him home, i'th'dark.

Here the play on words is established in the second line: the linguistic analogy between pimples and the Pleiades provides the basis upon which the "turn" of the final couplet is constructed. Patrick notes that an allusion may be made to Pimpla, "a hill and fountain sacred to

16. See, for instance, the banter of Clerimont and Truewit which is occasioned by the page's singing of the famous "Still to be neat, still to be drest" (*Epicoene* I.i).

the Muses," but that allusion functions only in terms of the "wheales" as small "hills" on Tom's face; it does not effect the "turn" of the poem. The pimples-Pleiades analogy, on the other hand, is functional: as the constellation shines at night, so Tom's pimples "shine" when he is "lit" from drinking beer.

A unique feature of this poem is the speaker's absolute withdrawal from the situation. It is not even his analogy, for Tom himself sets it up and Tom himself draws the conclusion. The incongruity of the analogy, the beautiful and transcendent constellation compared to a rather earthy and almost grotesque feature, gains ironic force simply because it is Tom's rather than an omniscient observer's.

A more traditional kind of word-play provides the "turn" in "To a Maid" (H-317):

> YOu say, you love me; that I thus must prove;
> If that you lye, then I will sweare you love.

The joke depends upon the pun on "lye." "Lye" can be taken first as simple verbal deception, in which case the point of the poem is the paradoxical nature of love and the "proof" mentioned in the first line is a dialectical testing. But "lye" also carries obvious sexual implications, in which case the "proof" is decidedly more physical. The poem is sheer sport, little more than a courtly or Cavalier display of wit.

"Upon Jack and Jill" (H-498) "discloses" the incompatibility of art and reality in a more expansive epigrammatic form:

> WHen *Jill* complaines to *Jack* for want of meate;
> *Jack* kisses *Jill*, and bids her freely eate:
> *Jill* sayes, of what? sayes *Jack*, on that sweet kisse,
> Which full of Nectar and Ambrosia is,
> The food of Poets; so I thought sayes *Jill*,
> That makes them looke so lanke, so Ghost-like still.
> Let Poets feed on aire, or what they will;
> Let me feed full, till that I fart, sayes *Jill*.

There is no justification for trying to convert this witty poem into a philosophical and dialectical apologia for the "real" as opposed to the "artistic." The poem is simply a game, a parody of the lover-poet. Some of the humor comes from Jill's earthy demand and her equally earthy response to Jack's literally absurd proposal. But some of it also comes from the parody itself, which jokingly turns the poem into an anti-poetic, anti-Cavalier statement. There is a real sense of vitality about Jill, a vitality which is enforced on the one hand by the plain and blunt language of the final line, and on the other by being paired with the very "unreal" approach of Jack. To read the poem, as some have done, as embodying a philosophical tension rather than as a plain parody of a hyperbolic situation is to miss all the humor here. In many of these poems Herrick shows himself to be a consummate humorist and his poems are quite simply great fun. In this sense, the sportive epigrams again point to the need for a comprehensive treatment of Herrick's wit throughout the volume. The sense of humor which places poems of widely differing genres, personae, and intentions side by side, which scatters poems on death and burial amid passionate-shepherd love-lyrics, and which shimmers underneath the surface of practically every poem in whatever genre, gives to the *Hesperides* a vitality and liveliness which have not yet been appreciated or documented.

In "The Thythe. To the Bride" (H-581), as in "Upon Judith" and "Upon Zelot," Herrick exploits the ironic application of religious matter to earthy subject:

> IF nine times you your Bride-groome kisse;
> The tenth you know the Parsons is.
> Pay then your Tythe; and doing thus,
> Prove in your Bride-bed numerous.
> If children you have ten, Sir *John*
> Won't for his tenth part ask you one.

The joke depends here on a twofold application of the tithing principle to the bride-bridegroom relationship, including a rather suggestive implication in the final two lines which is clarified by comparison with Herrick's ostensible source.[17] The joke is immeasurably height-

17. Although the precise form of the joke is a bit different in Herrick's

ened if Herrick is visualized in his country vicarage sporting with the young couple before or after the wedding ceremony. This bit of momentary fancifulness is not necessarily irrelevant, as the epigram does have a certain "homey" touch (note the addition Herrick makes to Heywood's poem in line four—a revealing bit of rustic superstition) and the speaker seems less detached than in the preceding examples.

All of the epigrams examined thus far are exercises in wit: they are not serious poems and they seek primarily to engage the reader in the joke, to make him laugh. In them Herrick seems to be giving in to what is firm and vital and real. That he treats this "reality" in epigrammatic form implies his desire to fix it in as permanent a state as he can; Batt and his peers are all frozen in memorable and characteristic actions. For the poet, this act of memorializing specific individuals becomes a literal ritual. And in this sense, the ostensible subject of the poem (Batt and the others) is not as important as the manner in which that subject is re-created poetically in a definitive and static form. The realistic ceremonial, in other words, defines here the process of the poetry rather than an aspect of the product.

At the far end of the scale of sportive epigrams is a group which represents a bridge of sorts between those which can be termed witty and those which have been called vulgar. "Upon Raspe" (H-400) is a convenient example:

> *RAspe* playes at Nine-holes;* and 'tis known he gets
> Many a Teaster** by his game, and bets:
> But of his gettings there's but little sign;
> When one hole wasts more then he gets by Nine.

[*"game of throwing small balls into nine holes"; **a coin—Patrick's notes]

---

version, his poem is strikingly similar to John Heywood's "An account of a mans children":

> Wyfe, of ten babes betwene vs by encrease growne,
> Thou saist I haue but nyne. no mo of your owne.
> Of all thynges encresyng, as my conscience lythe,
> The parson must needes haue the tenth for the tythe.

(*The fifth hundred of Epygrams*, No. 27 [1562]—quoted in *John Heywood's Works and Miscellaneous Short Poems*, ed. Burton A. Milligan, *Illinois Studies in Language and Literature* 41 [1956]: 210).

The poem is not vulgar, although the emphasis on "holes" may border on vulgarity. The play of wit, however, overshadows other implications. The final line might be taken in two ways: either Raspe's spendthrift wife wastes his gains or Raspe spends all of his winnings on his whore. Both readings provide legitimate points for satire, but satire obviously blunted in its seriousness by the verbal play on the court game. Nonetheless, the persona does seem to be approaching satiric intentions.

"The Custard" (H-131) is a step further removed from the merely sportive:

> FOr second course, last night, a Custard came
> To th'board, so hot, as none co'd touch the same:
> *Furze*, three or foure times with his cheeks did blow
> Upon the Custard, and thus cooled so:
> It seem'd by this time to admit the touch;
> But none co'd eate it, 'cause it stunk so much.

The element of wit is still primary here (note that Herrick is as clever as Jonson in assigning names to his subjects), although the speaker is getting closer to a delight in the grotesque which, in this case, would constitute vulgarity. This is but one of Herrick's many epigrams on "stinking" breath. Admittedly an obnoxious subject, it is difficult to explain why so many poems are devoted to it. John Kimmey has recently argued that Herrick writes as a satiric moralist in these poems, that "Breath, the spirit of man, evokes more vividly than any other aspect of his body, the decay deep within."[18] This assertion is an extension of Kimmey's basic thesis that Herrick's satire is "somewhere between the crude invective of the Elizabethan satirists and the brittle ironies of the Augustans," and that it concentrates on three weaknesses of man—his physical imperfections, his social or professional foibles, and his spiritual sin.[19] Historically, it is hard to disagree with this reading of the epigrams and Kimmey makes a strong case for it; but the question of Herrick's ostensibly *satiric* intentions still plagues the

18. "Robert Herrick's Satirical Epigrams," p. 314.
19. Kimmey, "Herrick's Satirical Epigrams," p. 313.

modern reader. The problem can perhaps be put in terms of the placement of these poems within the *Hesperides*. They do not exist as a self-contained group, but rather as frequent counterpoint to other kinds of poems. Such interlacing would seem to place more emphasis on humor and release than on moralistic satire.

The problem is even more complicated if we admit the existence of some clearly vulgar epigrams.[20] Vulgarity is, of course, difficult to define. It is more than obnoxious material. The vulgar epigrams concentrate on the grotesque, actually delight in the grotesque, not for the purpose of effecting a comic reversal or a joke, but simply for immersion in physical distortion. The danger Herrick faces in these poems can be phrased in Aristotelian terms, for human misery or disfiguration cannot be used as a comic theme. Physical grotesquerie can be used, as Kimmey and others suggest, to demonstrate inner, moral corruption, but such corruption, with its external manifestation, is a satiric subject, not a comic one. The justification for these poems depends, then, on the reader's ability to discern a satiric intent. Such an intent is, however, almost impossible to find: these poems show little moral point and no satiric indignation; they are simply a presentation of the grotesque divorced from all other considerations.

"Upon Blanch (H-99) is a fairly innocuous instance of the problems involved in such poems:

> *BLanch* swears her Husband's lovely; when a scald
> Has blear'd his eyes: Besides, his head is bald.
> Next, his wilde eares, like Lethern wings full spread,
> Flutter to flie, and beare away his head.

20. Since these "vulgar" epigrams are the ones which have most offended critics, it is important to notice that they represent a very small percentage of the total number of epigrams in the volume. According to my own figures, the vulgar epigrams number 16 out of a body of 620. Cf. Delattre's list of 59 epigrams, of which he says: "Les épigrammes forment comme une galerie où abondent les détails répugnants . . . toutes les horreurs en un mot de la pauvre bête humaine, étalées avec complaisance" (*Robert Herrick*, p. 148). His number is considerably larger than my own because of his tendency to include any poem dealing with a physical characteristic. Thus, "Upon Franck" (H-578): "*FRanck* ne'r wore silk she sweares; But I reply,/ She now weares silk to hide her blood-shot eye" is seen by Delattre as offensive. His list is thus a distortion of the size of this "gallery of grotesquerie."

Actually, the poem is not "Upon Blanch" at all, but on her husband, and is constructed of a series of rapidly flashing images: inflamed eyes, bald head, flapping ears, and a flying head. There is a progressive grotesquerie here, but nothing ties the images together except that all contradict Blanch's claim that her husband is "lovely." The portrait is far from a pretty one and could conceivably be intended to illustrate either the discrepancy between what the lover sees and what is actually there, or the relationship between affection and the perception of physical beauty. This would, indeed, give the poem a comic and ironic point, were it clearly the case. The mere piling up of the grotesque images could then reinforce the comedy of the portrait, for hyperbole is in this sense comic. But that very accumulation of images detracts in a distressing way from both the comedy and the irony. The poem turns into a one-sided medieval flyting in which abuse is heaped on abuse for no other reason than simple insult. There is no moral point here, no real thematic unity, and no legitimate reason for the scathing attack.

"Upon Jollies wife" (H-163) deals in the same kind of grotesque accretion:

> FIrst, *Jollies* wife is lame; then next, loose-hipt:
> Squint-ey'd, hook-nos'd; and lastly, Kidney-lipt.

Again we must question the justification, moral or otherwise, for this reveling in abhorrent physical details. Kimmey implies a serious point to the poem by noting the similarity of the description to Burton's definition of a vulgar woman in the *Anatomy of Melancholy*. The parallel is valuable, but Herrick's context and his larger intentions do not seem equivalent to Burton's. If the poem is examined "new-critically" and "loose-hipt" is read as a suggestion that Jolly's wife is a whore, then we begin to approach a moral justification. But the point is that that justification is not allowed to stand and is given no emphasis in the poem. The caesural pauses here, vastly outnumbering those in either the typical sportive or the gnomic epigrams, tend to place equal weight on each adjective in the appositive series and preclude our reading "loose-hipt" as any more or less significant than "hook-nos'd." Comedy and satire go by the board and we are left with the mere piling up of grotesque features solely for their own sake. The work is describable only in terms already used: a reveling in abhorrent accretion without moral, satiric, or comic point.

A concentration similar to, though more obnoxious than, the poet's on "stinking" breath is that on "corrupt" eyes. Two poems will illustrate—"Upon Loach" (H-816) and "Upon Reape" (H-879):

> SEal'd up with Night-gum, *Loach* each morning lyes,
> Till his Wife licking, so unglews his eyes.
> No question then, but such a lick is sweet,
> When a warm tongue do's with such Ambers meet.

$$* \quad * \quad *$$

> *REapes* eyes so rawe are, that (it seemes) the flyes
> Mistake the flesh, and flye-blow* both his eyes;
> So that an Angler, for a daies expence,
> May baite his hooke, with maggots taken thence.

[*"putrefy, by laying their eggs to hatch there"—Patrick's note]

In the first poem the grotesque features of the opening lines seem to give way to the less specific and more gentle irony of the final couplet, even though this couplet in no way mitigates the gruesome detail. The second poem does not provide a single relief. No satire is evident in either poem, no point or justification is used to make the presentation valid or necessary, and no attempt is made to lessen the offensiveness of the material. It is hard, in these poems, to disagree with McEuen's assertion that "satire, in its real sense of giving instruction by castigating persons guilty of infraction of moral, social, or literary laws, is not found in Herrick's poetry."[21]

It is necessary to be clear about why these poems are vulgar. In a society which accepts constant advertisements on bad breath, sweaty underarms, body odors of all kinds, facial blemishes, and the like, it cannot be simply the matter of these poems which offends. It is rather the seeming delight which the speaker takes in presenting these gruesome subjects. In addition, there is also the suspicion that he is trying

21. *Classical Influence upon the Tribe of Ben*, pp. 49–50.

to get us to participate in this experience of the grotesque even though we may not want to. By removing all justification for the specific details he allows no escape from literal and actual participation. The constant bombardment of horrors serves only to draw us further and further into this chaotic realm of physical distortion. At this point Ross's thesis that Herrick is here deliberately opposing the idyllic portraits which he draws in the pastorals, is "disclosing" the loathsome nature of our existence, becomes more appealing. Ross is correct in emphasizing the opposition between these particular epigrams and the pastorals, but the intent is not satiric "disclosure." Herrick's intentions seem closer to simply an immersion in plain, brutal fact, a giving in to what is literal and incontrovertible. In the pastoral poems he has been forced to concede certain qualifying facts or realities of existence and that concession yields uncertainty concerning the value of the pastoral ethos. The same process occurs in the courtly poems. One way beyond these uncertainties is simply to turn to the more conclusive, more definitive, view of existence pictured in these epigrams. This is not to say that the reality depicted here is the reality Herrick literally experiences or believes in. This "reality" is as conscious an artistic construction as that in the pastorals. This conception may help to explain Herrick's *use* of such poems in the volume as a whole, for their vulgarity may, in fact, be mitigated by the poet's utilitarian purpose in presenting them.

ii. THE GNOMIC VOICE

In order to understand fully what Herrick is about in both groups of sportive epigrams, it is necessary to examine the gnomic or sententious ones as well. These epigrams again present a detached observer who is superior in his attitude and definitive in his pronouncements. As opposed to the generally mimetic sportive epigrams, however, these are typically aphoristic and didactic: they seek to convert proverbial lore, regardless of its source, into concise and absolute dicta, or to transform private thought into proverbial form. Practically all of Herrick's gnomic poems fall under four major headings: those on the general state of man, those on the rules of right living, those on the rules of right government, and those on more aesthetic or emotional abstractions. In each group the persona is concerned less with wit than with presenting an absolute statement about the "few and simple truths" of human existence. At times the truths are sarcastic, sometimes even cynical, but they are always certain and definitive.

The epigrams on the general state of man are in some ways the most important of the gnomic poems, for in them Herrick lays the foundation for the rest of his *sententiae*. The vast majority of these poems deals with one basic motif—man's subjection to time. These epigrams are, therefore, a restatement in definitive terms of the qualifying notes sounded in the pastoral and courtly lyrics. But there is a significant difference: in those lyrics, time, mutability, and death were seen as merely *qualifying* aspects of man's state, even though the qualification is very strong; here, these facts are not only primary, but absolute and irrevocable. Herrick takes in these poems a step beyond the pastoral and courtly lyrics into a realm in which mutability and death are the controlling forces and in which man's chief task is simply to recognize this fact. The realm of the gnomic epigram presents little chance of escape because it ostensibly mirrors the very reality which surrounds man. The speaker, as well as the reader, is forced to confront the tenuity of his existence. For this reason, the tone of these poems is perfectly serious, at times even somber, because the reality they define is hardly consoling.

Perhaps the boldest statement of the principal attitude in these poems occurs in "Putrefaction" (H-432):

> PUtrefaction is the end
> Of all that Nature doth entend.

A literal paraphrase of the poem suggests that the final state of all natural objects is decay. But "entend" also implies purpose, in which case the paraphrase carries a more cynical tone: "the ultimate purpose of all natural objects is to decay or rot." Either reading produces a shock, in part because of the Latinate "Putrefaction," in part because of the definitiveness and the bluntness of the assertion. It does little good to speak of the persona's detachment here, for the emotional force behind the pronouncement is a strong and cynical one. The poem obviously gives voice to a powerfully felt antipathy to this "end" of the natural process. Some readers have objected that the poem refers only to nature itself, not to man, but this is hardly the case since most of the intensity of the epigram comes from the speaker's (and the reader's) realization that he too is a part of this "natural" state. In terms of "Putrefaction," the human-natural correspondence is total. In a later epigram Herrick strengthens the identification:

> THe body's salt, the soule is; which when gon,
> The flesh soone sucks in putrifaction.

> (H-1111)

The graphic image of the final line overshadows the Christian implications of the first and the verb "sucks in" emphasizes both the speed and the finality of the putrefying "end." [22] The only difference in this respect between man and plants or animals is that man knows what his true end will be.

Herrick extends this human-natural correspondence in several other mutability epigrams, especially in a series based upon a tree analogy. The basis of the analogue is established in "All things decay and die" (H-69):

> *ALL things decay with Time*: The Forrest sees
> The growth, and down-fall of her aged trees:
> That Timber tall, which three-score *lusters* stood
> The proud *Dictator* of the State-like wood:
> I meane (the Soveraigne of all Plants) the Oke
> Droops, dies, and falls without the cleavers stroke.

Nature provides images of literal truth and, like the later Romantic seer, the speaker here reads in the natural objects surrounding him the lessons of his own mortality. He does not hesitate to apply what he learns:

22. Kimmey asserts that "putrifaction" in this poem does not mean death but "moral decay and degeneration" (*"Herrick's Satirical Epigrams,"* pp. 313–14).

> ONe of the five straight branches of my hand
> Is lopt already; and the rest but stand
> Expecting when to fall: which soon will be;
> First dyes the Leafe, the Bough next, next the tree.
>
> (H-565)
>
> DIe ere long I'm sure, I shall;
> After leaves, the tree must fall.
>
> (H-1058)

In the first poem the three-line situation is capped off by the natural analogy in the final line, an analogy which recounts in chronological order the true lesson of nature: *"All things decay with Time."* The emotional impact of these epigrams is not as forceful as that of the "Putrefaction" ones, partly because the detachment is not qualified by suspicion of a covert indignation and partly because the analogy itself tends to obviate strict attention to the end result—death. But this end is nonetheless vivid in the speaker's mind and provides the basis for the comparison in the first place. Man can be certain about only one act in his life—the act of dying.

Because time is the governing factor of mutability, a logical analogue for man's state is "The Watch" (H-558):

> MAn is a Watch, wound up at first, but never
> Wound up again: Once down, He's down for ever.
> The Watch once downe, all motions then do cease;
> And Mans Pulse stopt, *All passions sleep in Peace.*

Here the oppressive nature of change is blunted by the generality of the depiction and by the substitution of the euphemistic "down for ever" and *"sleep in Peace"* for more forceful expressions of the same point. The poem does continue the emphasis of these epigrams in that all intermediate moments are omitted: the watch is wound up and the watch stops; man is born and man dies—all time between these acts is inconsequential.

Two more epigrams on the general state of man again demonstrate Herrick's confrontation with the forces against him:

ALl things o'r-rul'd are here by Chance;
The greatest mans Inheritance,
Where ere the luckie Lot doth fall,
Serves but for place of Buriall.

(H-542)

TIme is the Bound of things, where e're we go,
Fate gives a meeting. Death's the end of woe.

(H-766)

Time and Chance, Death and Burial—these are the key terms in the gnomic poems dealing with man's condition. The speaker faces directly the challenge raised in the pastoral and courtly lyrics only fleetingly. He forces himself, and his readers, to view the bleak realities of existence, especially in the second poem where the progressively terrifying movement from Time, to Fate, to Death yields not only a sense of ominous and imminent doom, but a concise finality as well. These epigrams, in a sense, are to the other lyrics of the *Hesperides* what the book of Ecclesiastes is to the Song of Solomon.

As stated above, those epigrams which deal with man's general condition consider only two phases of his life, birth and death. The emphasis, of course, is almost exclusively on the latter. In the group of poems dealing with the rules of right living, the gnomic persona fills in the void by outlining the principles governing man's life between birth and death.[23] But these principles are very general and the picture of man given in the poems is a vague and blurred one because he is always portrayed in ideal rather than real situations. Part of the haziness of the rules of right living is caused by the persona's falling back on conventional Christian arguments which, by their very conventionality, do not require precise delineation. It might also be added that this group of epigrams contains the most explicitly Christian sentiments of the *Hesperides*. Unlike most of the poems in the volume, which *use* Christian elements for other purposes (e.g., heightening,

23. Rollin is surely right when he directs our attention to how these poems fulfill the Jonsonian dictum that poetry must offer "a certain rule and Patterne of living well, and happily" (*Robert Herrick*, p. 82).

sanctifying, broadening the context, and so forth), these poems simply expound a rather facile and didactic Christian message. Not all of the poems in this group are so blatantly Christian, however; some deal with more classical exhortations concerning the good life or the right way to enjoy life (e.g., you get back what you put in; the wise man is the moderate man; live within your means). In the latter class, right living is equatable not with "virtuous" living but with "free" living—an enjoying of the time or times.[24]

The best example of the Christian rules is "The Christian Militant" (H-323):

> A Man prepar'd against all ills to come,
> That dares to dead the fire of martirdome:
> That sleeps at home; and sayling there at ease,
> Feares not the fierce sedition of the Seas:
> That's counter-proofe against the Farms mis-haps,
> Undreadfull too of courtly thunderclaps:
> That weares one face (like heaven) and never showes
> A change, when Fortune either comes, or goes:
> That keeps his own strong guard, in the despight
> Of what can hurt by day, or harme by night:
> That takes and re-delivers every stroake
> Of Chance, (as made up all of rock, and oake:)
> That sighs at others death; smiles at his own
> Most dire and horrid crucifixion.
> Who for true glory suffers thus; we grant
> Him to be here our *Christian militant*.

It is a curious poem, similar to the pastoral vision and even the stock imagery of "A Country life." But the point of view is drastically altered. Whereas the reward of a certain kind of living in the pastoral vision is contentment, serenity, and happiness, here the same life insures but "suffering" and "martirdome." The keynote of the militant's character and life is preparedness: regardless of what happens to him, he is always ready to do battle against any ills. The poem is an elaborate

24. Rollin, *Robert Herrick*, pp. 81–84.

and documented definition whose working condition is the conception of Chance or Fortune (the two seem synonymous here). It gives one possible answer, therefore, to the challenge mutability poses: the Boethian answer that a truly righteous man neither fears nor is anxious about changes in his condition or his fortune.[25] He is impervious to the very transience of things and suffers all (in the sense of accepts all) for the sake of "true glory" or life everlasting:

> IN the hope of ease to come,
> Let's endure one Martyrdome.
>
> (H-1027)

The picture is a serene and reassuring one: the martyrdom of this life is a preparation for, almost a guarantee of, the reward of ease and peace in the eternal life to follow. And the Christian persona makes certain the point is not missed:

> EAch must, in vertue, strive for to excell;
> *That man lives twice, that lives the first life well.*
>
> (H-298)

The proverb of the final line, taken from Martial,[26] usually refers not to Christian afterlife, but to the ability of the virtuous man to enjoy both his present moments and the satisfied memory of past moments. There can be little doubt, however, that the Christian interpretation is intended here. The context in which the poem must be viewed appears more clearly in "The Plaudite, or end of life" (H-225):

> IF after rude and boystrous seas,
> My wearyed Pinnace here finds ease:
> If so it be I've gain'd the shore
> With safety of a faithful Ore:
> If having run my Barque on ground,
> Ye see the aged Vessell crown'd:
> What's to be done? but on the Sands

25. See *The Consolation of Philosophy* IV. Prose 7, p. 99.
26. *Epigrammata*, X.23.7–8. See the two translations noted by Patrick, both of which reveal the limited scope of Martial's concept in comparison to Herrick's expansion of it.

> Ye dance, and sing, and now clap hands.
> The first Act's doubtfull, (but we say)
> It is the last commends the Play.

The appeal is for salvation after a weary and long "martirdome." The play is existence: the first act is life on earth; the last is the final judgment and eternal life in heaven. Herrick has gone far beyond any account of death. In fact, death does not exist for this persona; his only reality is that of eternal life in a typically serene and peaceful Christian heaven.

All of these poems seek the same answer to the problem of death: if a man lives virtuously, he will be rewarded with immortality. It is, in a sense, the same answer Herrick's self-assured persona will give in the *Noble Numbers*. In that book, however, the assumed naïveté, the childlike ingenuous role, and the absolute certainty with which the Christian answer is given do not jar with any other context. Here the tone of these epigrams seems more forced; the answer is too affirmative in the face of conflicting tones, too oversimplified in the light of the other epigrams and lyrics. Second, by providing only a very small number of such poems Herrick qualifies the answer they give. Those who have called Herrick a pagan poet are right insofar (and probably *only* this far) as the Christian didactic statements of the *Hesperides* must be seen as but another attempt to reach a definitive answer to the poet's most disturbing problem. The very fact that his Christian epigrams treat man at his most ideal rather than most real state also makes them less convincing, less emotionally powerful, and less sincere than the other epigrams. They represent a falling back by the persona to the certain and relatively simplified (because escapist) conclusions of an optimistic Christianity.

To clarify these points we need only look at three other epigrams on the rules of right living which deal with a different, and in some ways opposing, answer to the problem of time. The first is "To live Freely" (H-453):

> LEt's live in hast; use pleasures while we may:
> Co'd life return, 'twod never lose a day.

This is the traditional *carpe diem* exhortation, but the injunction is given firm support not only by the pastoral and courtly lyrics but also by the epigrams on man's general condition. The poem refuses to ignore the fact of death, as the Christian ones do, and faces death squarely to suggest at least one plausible approach to it. And while this approach does not rid the speaker of the problem, it does present a more specific and a more honest answer to the question of how man should live his life.

"To enjoy the Time" (H-457) continues in this classical vein:

> WHile Fate permits us, let's be merry;
> Passe all we must the fatall Ferry:
> And this our life too whirles away,
> With the Rotation of the Day.

Ostensibly, the answer here is the same as that in the preceding poem, but there is an even stronger acknowledgment of the oppressive force of time. Because the epigram recognizes this fact, and because the view agrees with that in the poems on man's condition, the *carpe diem* solution seems more in line with the emotional tenor of this persona, more congruent with the reader's expectations of him, than the Christian answer. It is also important to note that although the *carpe diem* injunction appears in a great many of Herrick's poems, it is raised to its ultimate level of a motive for human action of all kinds only in these aphoristic epigrams.

In "To Youth" (H-655) Herrick combines the *carpe diem* motif with a Bacchanalian call to frolic:

> DRink Wine, and live here blithefull, while ye may:
> *The morrowes life too late is, Live to day.*

If the epigram is of any importance at all to Herrick, it is an attempt to grasp and present what is real, and to reproduce that reality in undeniable, unquestionable terms. It is their apparent lack of concern with reality that condemns the Christian epigrams of this group to a less vital and less significant position than the classical ones.

The third group of gnomic epigrams demands less attention than the first two primarily because it contains the most stereotyped and repetitious, as well as the fewest, poems. These epigrams deal with the rules of right government and are divided equally between straight-forward representations of fact and hortatory appeals. In both cases the poems are royalist, though not always blindly optimistic about the nature of kingship or the character of the king. Still, the essential thesis of this group of epigrams is that man as a whole is an unmanageable and unruly lot unless a strong king and strong laws contain him. "The Difference Betwixt Kings and Subjects" (H-25) shows this premise at its simplest level:

> TWixt Kings and Subjects ther's this mighty odds,
> Subjects are taught by *Men*; Kings by the *Gods*.

The epigram is royalist in the true Cavalier tradition: the king is the divinely appointed sovereign of the people and is accountable to the Divinity alone. The people's duty lies in recognizing and accepting the king's sacred authority.[27] The poem in no way qualifies the defin-itiveness of its statement: the speaker is serious and authoritarian, and the reader must accept the truth of the dogmatic assertion. The apho-ristic form, in which the relationship between sovereign and subject is examined through denotative definition, is the most common one in Herrick's governmental epigrams.

In "Duty to Tyrants" (H-97) the royalist persona goes a step be-yond the preceding poem:

> GOod Princes must be pray'd for: for the bad
> They must be borne with, and in rev'rence had.
> Doe they first pill thee, next, pluck off thy skin?
> *Good children kisse the Rods, that punish sin.*
> Touch not the Tyrant; Let the Gods alone
> To strike him dead, that but usurps a Throne.

Here the subjects are bound even to an unlawful king and he is ac-countable to none but God. It is an old plea (though the speaker's

27. For a comprehensive discussion of the Cavalier attitude toward kingship, as well as some representative figures and poems, see Delattre, *Robert Herrick*, pp. 123–37.

attitude toward his audience, the "children," cannot be described as
a "plea": he is the stern father warning of dire consequences should
the evil act be committed) and assumes an old set of values.[28] Although
it is unlikely that the poem is written to fellow royalists after the
Parliamentary forces had gained control, it is easy to believe it directed
to those forces at the beginning of their struggle. It reinvokes the political system of the medieval and Elizabethan Chain of Being, especially the doctrine of "degree"—a doctrine and a system obviously
faltering by the 1630's. And while it is hardly possible to agree with
those who see Herrick as living in an Elizabethan dream world, oblivious of the revolutionary events of the times, there is a strong sense
of pathos in the attempt to call back a rapidly receding past and the
rational system which gave that past coherence and order. But the
point is that Herrick invokes the older Elizabethan system simply because it *is* static—it is certain, understandable, rational, ordered. And,
as suggested earlier, it is perfectly natural that Herrick should present
these "certainties" in the epigrammatic form, for its very finality and
aphoristic precision denies any destructive or disordering elements. The
epigram, by nature, appeals to long-established ideals. The desire for
control, for surety and definitive pronouncement, which causes this
persona to invoke a specific hierarchical system of political stations,
also causes him to choose an epigrammatic form to express the system.

"Ill Government" (H-536) illustrates the more cynical attitude
of this persona:

> PReposterous is that Government, (and rude)
> When Kings obey the wilder Multitude.

The sensitive reader of Herrick's verse is struck immediately by the
words "rude" and "wilder." Whenever Herrick castigates or rails
against a person or a group of people, regardless of the events involved
or the persona used, "rude" is practically the strongest word he can
find. Remember, for instance, that Dean-bourn is a "rude" river and
that its people are "rude (almost) as rudest Salvages." Similarly, al-

---

28. Cf. Delattre's assertion that Herrick invokes old politics to solve new
problems (*Robert Herrick*, p. 135–36).

though "wild" may be perfectly acceptable in a person or an object, as in "wilde civility," "wilder" always points to an undesirable excess. Whether or not the poem has any relation to the civil disorders in England, it presents a disparaging and cynical attitude toward mankind. Only when men are under the firm and forceful control of the king can there be any responsible or workable government. At this point the persona is approaching Machiavellianism, but full-fledged adoption of that position does not come until poems like "A King and no King" (H-1103):

> THat Prince, who may doe nothing but what's just,
> Rules but by leave, and takes his Crowne on trust.

The implications here are both obvious and bitter. The king *needs* to be above the usual moral laws, for any attempt on his part to be purely honest or just will allow the unjust and dishonest factions of the multitude to overthrow him. For a Cavalier in the 1630's, the horror of civil chaos was obviously increasing, and it bred a correspondingly militant form of royalism.

In all of these epigrams on right government, Herrick is again engaged in the ceremony of realism, although "realism" is often equatable here with a cynical pragmatism. Regardless of the descriptive terms used to define the poems, they are attempts to present dogmatically a self-contained and self-assured system of beliefs. They are a falling back on what is unquestionable and the authoritarian manner in which they are expressed argues the urgency of the appeal. In many ways, these epigrams, like those already discussed, illustrate that Herrick is indeed a typical seventeenth-century poet, a poet attempting to grasp with fervor whatever is solid, whatever can be held onto, whatever provides a dogmatic certainty and reasonableness in a chaotic and disintegrating age.

The final group of gnomic epigrams is, in some respects, the most interesting of all Herrick's poems in the genre, first because it is more varied in subject matter, and second, because its poems frequently display a lightness of touch not always evident in the other groups.

The speaker here seems less self-assertive, although the definitions he gives and the pronouncements he makes are still assured and final. With this group we return to the Herrick of delightful miniatures, for there is a freedom about these epigrams noticeably absent from the others: cynicism disappears, vulgarity is avoided, didactic preaching toned down. Herrick returns to a realm of affirmation, of joy, sweetness, and gaiety. For these reasons it is a bit disappointing that this series of poems is no larger than it is.

Two short poems on love provide a convenient entry into a survey of these epigrams. The first is "Love what it is" (H-29):

> LOve is a circle that doth restlesse move
> In the same sweet eternity of love.

As Patrick notes, the thought comes from Burton's *Anatomy* (3.1.1.2), in which love is described as *"Circulus à bono in bonum,* a round circle still from good to good." Herrick does two unique things with the idea. The first involves a kind of "circular" argument: love is a circle within a greater circle of love. The former is earthly and time bound, human and ever changing, secondary and actual; the latter is heavenly and eternal, divine and immutable, primary and potential. Yet each embodies and mirrors the other. The poem evokes a whole panorama of implications, most of which have been recovered by Marjorie Nicolson in *The Breaking of the Circle.* And the poem gains in effectiveness when we note that the "circle" of its definition is mirrored in the "circle" of its syntax.

The second interesting feature has largely been described above although not named: the use of a single word, "restlesse," to define love in the first, or human, sense and to distinguish it from love in the second, or divine, sense. Philosophically, *eros* is distinguished from *agape.* All of the poem's emotion is contracted into this one word, though it would be impossible to describe adequately just how this occurs or even what the emotion is. The choice of the word is governed by a keen sense of the ever-striving, ever-changing, ever-seeking to be fulfilled and to fulfil nature of earthly love, and how such love relates to the more comprehensive and binding universal love, the Chain of Love, in the Boethian sense.[29] Whatever the explanation, we intuitively celebrate the felicity of the word choice.

A definition of more conventional scope can be found in "Another on Love" (H-1084):

> LOve's of it self, too sweet; the best of all
> Is, when loves hony has a dash of gall.

Although the poem is based on the stock antithesis of sweetness and bitterness, the connection of these adjectives to the state of love carries with it innumerable associations and feelings. The interplay between these feelings, these memories perhaps of past experiences, accomplishes the purpose of the epigram—to define love as a "combination" of bittersweet emotions. The idea is hardly a new one, but the presentation is distinctive and effective. Moreover, it raises the concept of a "mean" which occurs also in the pastoral poems, an explicit denial of excess on either side and a call for an intermediate point.

This conception of a "mean" arises frequently in these epigrams and usually signals a certain level of awareness on the part of the persona, a sensitivity which the reader affirms and applauds. "Soft Musick" (H-24) is a good example:

> THe mellow touch of musick most doth wound
> The soule, when it doth rather sigh, then sound.

The reference to "wounding" the soul suggests that the emotional state here is close to melancholy, but the thought extends beyond this limited mood and encompasses all musical ranges. It is not necessary to agree with the idea in order to acknowledge its validity. The reference is to a "mean" of musical volume, but includes implicitly a "mean" of emotional response as well.

In "The Definition of Beauty" (H-102) the doctrine of the "mean" is presented once more:

> BEauty, no other thing is, then a Beame
> Flasht out between the Middle and Extreame.

29. See *The Consolation of Philosophy* II, Poem 8, p. 41; IV, Poem 6, pp. 96–97.

The idea again finds a probable source in Burton's *Anatomy* (3.1.1.2):
"Beauty shines, Plato saith . . ." and "Beauty and grace are like those
beams and shinings that come from the glorious and divine sun." But
there is a problem here, both visually and aesthetically. To take the
latter first, it may be assumed that one extreme is ugliness; what, then,
is the other? That ultimate beauty suggested by the myth of Zeus and
Semele? If so, the implication is too obscure. Visually there is more
trouble, for the "beame" is between the middle and the extremes,
emanating, it would seem, from the middle. Since a span of light
widens as it gets farther from the source, the most beauty would lie at
the extremes, not in the middle as must be intended. In other words,
either the direction of the beam is here reversed, or beauty is the middle
point, not the beam at all. Or, does the figure refer to the "intensity"
of the beam at its smallest point? While acknowledging the possibilities of the analogy, the shaping of the figure must be termed inadequate.

A better definition of beauty occurs in "Beauty" (H-840):

> BEauti's no other but a lovely Grace
> Of lively colours, flowing from the face.

The "beame" image of the former poem is still present, but submerged,
and instead of signalling a "mean" of any sort it now represents a
contracted span of colors. The conjunction of the "beame" image,
which is here imaginary and abstract, with the woman's face, which
is real and specific, adds a vitality to the definition. The real achievement of the poem, however, lies in the control of sound patterns. The
liquid "l's" of "lovely" and "lively" tend to draw the two lines of
the poem together; the opposing vowel sounds of the same words keep
the lines distinctly apart. The capping of the conclusion by the three
"f" sounds completes the separation and places the emphasis on the
final visual image. This use of consonant and vowel sounds to support
and underscore meaning can be found throughout the *Hesperides* and
again argues for the sure self-consciousness of the artistry at work
here.[30]

30. A step towards defining the interrelationships between music and form
in Herrick's poetry has recently been taken by John Kimmey in "Order and

"Bashfulnesse" (H-300), our final poem of this group, is a perfect example of what is meant by calling Herrick a miniaturist:

> OF all our parts, the eyes expresse
> The sweetest kind of bashfulnesse.

The art of a "miniaturist" poet consists in taking the simplest of images or actions, such as a blinking of an eye, and transforming it into a meaningful experience in the smallest of spaces. The sentiment is delicate and gentle without being sentimental; the sensibility is refined and incisive. The reader responds intuitively and affirmatively to this kind of statement. His understanding and agreement allow him, indeed force him, to participate in the speaker's particular vision. But then again, this is inaccurate; it is not really the reader's understanding which forces this participation, but his emotional response. Once again the crux of the problem in so much of Herrick's poetry appears. The reader's emotional, not intellectual, response is the key element, for the poem invites celebration of a particular vision and sensibility by demonstrating them in action. Intuitive acceptance of the vision means that we too share the sensibility, although not necessarily the artistry to frame it into words.

As stated earlier, the epigrams in the *Hesperides* are used as a means of definitive pronouncement and as such may be described as a cere-monial of realism. Whether this realism is the depiction of the grotesque features of human bodies, of the foibles of particular caricatures, or of general laws governing human behavior and man's condition in this world, there is a total commitment to what is actual, or at least to what is presented as actual. Sometimes, it is true, this commitment is disastrous, as when deformity is made the brunt of attempted humor. But even here the persona is trying to construct something tangible, something certain about his existence. In the sportive epigrams the play of wit depends heavily on the reality of the situation presented. Whether mimetic or didactic, the poems seek to isolate and memori-

---

Form in Herrick's *Hesperides*." Much more needs to be done, however, for Herrick deserves the kind of close analysis now being given to Herbert, for example.

alize those facts of the human condition that are unquestionable and undebatable. As suggested at the beginning of this chapter, Herrick's epigrams are best viewed as "memorial inscriptions," as celebratory forms by which the poet attempts to transform private thoughts into public truths. Private thoughts, of course, and especially private perceptions, are subject to continual change; they can never be accepted as fixed or stabilized in any certain way. The public truths of an epigrammatic memorial, though, are both unqualified and unchangeable; their very permanence is their highest value for it alone defines their ultimate "truth."

There is one final group of epigrams which has been omitted from this discussion. The subject of most of these poems is either the poet himself or the book he is writing. In a sense, therefore, the poems of this group could be seen as the most important of the entire volume for in them Herrick tests all of his major presumptions about his art and the things it is capable of doing. That is, in these poems he subjects his private hopes for poetry to epigrammatic form in order to validate them. By proving that these hopes can be rendered as absolute truths, this group of epigrams leads Herrick to his ultimate celebration of the ritual of poetry itself, a rite explored in all its forms in the next chapter.

CHAPTER V

THE ARTISTIC
CEREMONIAL

THE POEMS to be discussed in this chapter can be seen, quite literally perhaps, as the thematic and poetic culmination of the *Hesperides*. All are concerned exclusively with mutability and all depend upon and proceed from the human condition defined in the pastoral, courtly, and realistic poems. The inevitability of death which continually qualifies the idyllic and urban visions is here confronted directly and made the basis of a new approach to reality. No longer exploring different mediums through which his ceremonial vision can be demonstrated, Herrick here subsumes his pastoral, courtly, and realistic voices under a more limited "artistic" or "poetic" one. He directs attention in these poems not to the rural, courtly, or epigrammatic features of a poet-singer, but to the strictly artistic qualities of that singer's song.

Likewise, the ceremony Herrick creates here is not to be seen as a primarily pastoral or courtly one, but as a *poetic* one. In the opening chapter it was suggested that Herrick's poetic ceremonial attempts to go beyond transience by creating a realm of artistic stasis through isolation of the fragmentary and seemingly inconsequential acts of ordinary life and through the transformation of those acts into a broader and more complete view of human existence. In the poems which follow, Herrick's transformation of dying and death into significant ritualistic actions heightens and intensifies the meaning of the poetic ceremonial and allows both poet and reader to transcend the insignificance of their ends.

The distinction between the *poetic* rites of the present group of poems and the pastoral or courtly rites of those already examined is problematic enough to require some recapitulation. In the lyrics discussed in Chapters II and III, Herrick frequently isolates and "represents" rites which literally exist outside the poem—the hock-cart festival, the May Day ritual, the courtly "wooing" games—and whose significance depends in part on their specifically country or city settings. As suggested, however, Herrick's "re-presentation" of these literal rites is itself ceremonial in form and intent. This "poetic" rite has no actual existence outside the poem and is limited to neither the pastoral nor the courtly worlds as it underlies both. In the epigrams analyzed in Chapter IV, Herrick does not "re-present" any literal rite like the hock-cart and his ceremony is rather the rhetorical treatment of the subject, the rite of definitive pronouncement. Nonetheless, these poems are not as different from the pastoral and courtly ones as their respective rituals might imply: the epigrams are characterized by the nature of the speaker, the realistic voice, just as the courtly poems are characterized by a Cavalier voice. In each instance, the specific qualities of the limited personae tend to overshadow and obscure the more abstract artistic ritual involved. In the lyrics and epigrams to be discussed in this chapter, the persona is literally the *poet* (not Robert Herrick, but a fictitious and conscious mask), even though he makes use of the pastoral, courtly, and epigrammatic forms. Therefore, the reader's attention is not directed in these poems to an external rite to which the lyric may allude, but to the ceremonial artistry creating and shaping that poem. The poem itself is the ceremony and participation in this ritual is the act of writing or reading the verse.

i. THE PASTORAL VOICE

The pastoral forms included in the "artistic ceremonial" are two, the burial instruction and the epitaph. Both, of course, confront death directly and seek to transcend it in their own special ways. As seen in Chapter II, the pastoral persona's total commitment to the pastoral life in general, or to certain pastoral rites in particular, engages him, and his readers, in another, more terrifying, commitment—to the inevitability of death as the end of the natural process. The pastoral persona cannot escape the latter commitment given his own terms. By means of the burial instruction and the epitaph, however, Herrick

alters those terms and tries again to transcend the natural end to which
he has by definition bound his pastoral voice.

   Although neither of these forms, "The Funerall Rites of the Rose"
(H-686) provides a convenient starting point for this discussion since
it demonstrates the essential features and intentions governing Herrick's burial poems.

> THe Rose was sick, and smiling di'd;
> And (being to be sanctifi'd)
> About the Bed, there sighing stood
> The sweet, and flowrie Sisterhood.
> Some hung the head, while some did bring
> (To wash her) water from the Spring.
> Some laid her forth, while other wept,
> But all a solemne Fast there kept.
> The holy Sisters some among
> The sacred *Dirge* and *Trentall* sung.
> But ah! what sweets smelt every where,
> As Heaven had spent all perfumes there.
> At last, when prayers for the dead,
> And Rites were all accomplished;
> They, weeping, spread a Lawnie Loome,
> And clos'd her up, as in a Tombe.

The most obvious feature of the poem is the personification of the
Rose and her compatriot flowers. Not simply personified, the flowers
are also deliberately transformed into religious figures by the imagery:
"sanctifi'd," "Sisterhood," "solemne Fast," "holy Sisters," "sacred
Dirge and *Trentall*," "Heaven," "prayers," and "Rites." On a literal
level, then, the poem heightens the significance of the Rose's death by
placing it in a nexus of religious association. The Rose becomes an
image of the Virgin, and the flowers surrounding the bed, or altar,
become sacrificing nuns. The death of the Rose is also heightened
in meaning because of the action it precipitates—the Sisterhood's ritual
of mourning.[1] The ritual, as line 2 suggests, sanctifies the Rose's

   1. See Deming's discussion of Herrick's "ritual of mourning" in "The

death by evoking and necessitating a precise public ceremony, as well as by providing the proper "conclusion" to her life.

On a more important level, however, the poem must be read as a process, for it depicts this ritual as primarily a function of art, or the poetry. The poem itself is the tomb of the Rose and the construction of the poem is the ritual of mourning described in it.[2] The sanctification here is something quite different: the beauty of the Rose is removed from the flux of nature to the static realm of art; the death of the Rose is elevated and given special importance by the *poetic* act it inspires. In this way death is not denied but transcended, though perhaps only for the duration of the poem itself. The artistic ceremonial, therefore, is not simply Herrick's use of classical rites in these poems, but the manner in which he uses a *poetic* ritual to construct an artistic stasis.

The process of artistic creation at work here is the same in virtually all the poems discussed in this chapter. The singing of specific aspects of experience heightens the significance of the subjects, sanctifies the song itself, and fixes the object of that song in a realm more integrated and more permanent than the natural one. By means of the artistic ceremonial, this realm is art itself.

"To Perilla" (H-14) is chronologically the first burial instruction in the *Hesperides* and indicative of the genre's typical form.

> AH my Perilla! do'st thou grieve to see
> Me, day by day, to steale away from thee?
> Age cals me hence, and my gray haires bid come,
> And haste away to mine eternal home;
> 'Twill not be long (*Perilla*) after this,
> That I must give thee the *supremest* kisse:

Classical Ceremonial," pp. 119–21. His conclusion regarding this poem is worth repeating: "Only ceremony is eternal and only the proper poetic ceremony can insure eternal significance" (p. 121). Elsewhere in the study Deming seems to reverse himself, however, by claiming that the ceremonial does not transcend death in any way. See note 4 below.

2. Whitaker, "Herrick and the Fruits of the Garden," p. 23; Deming, "Herrick's Funeral Poems," p. 157. It might be noted that Whitaker bases his entire essay on this poem and I am considerably indebted, here and elsewhere, to his reading.

> Dead when I am, first cast in salt, and bring
> Part of the creame from that *Religious Spring*;
> With which (*Perilla*) wash my hands and feet;
> That done, then wind me in that very sheet
> Which wrapt thy smooth limbs (when thou didst implore
> The Gods protection, but the night before)
> Follow me weeping to my Turfe, and there
> Let fall a *Primrose*, and with it a teare:
> Then lastly, let some weekly-strewings be
> Devoted to the memory of me:
> Then shall my *Ghost* not walk about, but keep
> Still in the coole, and silent shades of sleep.

The first part of the poem (ll. 1–6) is a complaint against transience and mutability; the second (ll. 7–18) is an exhortation to Perilla to carry out certain ritualistic actions. The exhortation is the focus of attention, though, and the speaker begins, in line 7, by asking for a preparation of his body to forestall the "putrefaction" which he observes in other poems immediately follows death. In lines 7–8 his body is purified (another form of preparation) by tears from Perilla's own eyes ("that *Religious Spring*"). Next, it is wrapt in a special winding sheet, again supplied by Perilla, and, in fact, the one in which she slept but the night before. (This surprising emphasis on a kind of ultimate union of the two lovers betrays a vein of the Cavalier wit in this primarily pastoral persona and may threaten the emotional consistency of his statement). Finally, the body is buried amid the typically Roman rites of weeping and weekly strewings.[3]

At least two things are evident in this section of the poem: the precisely ordered sequence of events and the care with which these actions are extended beyond the present moment. Both points are effective in establishing the ritualistic nature of Perilla's duties, and it is clear that her individual deeds are not as important as their sum total. The fact that they are recognized as part of a ritual itself height-

---

3. For classical analogues to this "ritual of mourning," see Tibullus, *Elegies* III.ii.9ff. and Propertius, *Elegies*, I. xix.23ff. See Deming, "The Classical Ceremonial," pp. 96–116; "Herrick's Funeral Poems," pp. 154–55, 158–59.

ens the meaning of the death which occasions that rite. Instead of a simple, natural fact, the speaker's death is now an event worth commemorating in ritualistic form.

Furthermore, the value of this ceremony is demonstrated by the speaker's consolation, as witnessed in the emotional shift from the opening tone of complaint to the calm serenity of the final two lines:

> Then shall my *Ghost* not walk about, but keep
> Still in the coole, and silent shades of sleep.

As long as the ritual of mourning, complete with tears and strewings, is periodically re-enacted, it continually invokes remembrance of the speaker and continually elevates the significance of his death. But this is not an actual ritual: it is a speaker pleading for one. The plea is consoling only insofar as he can construct a rite to transcend his own end. His *poetic* construction creates the stasis of celebratory affirmation, a stasis in which he is always just dying and Perilla is always mourning. Significantly, this poetic ceremonial places the lonely and solitary act of dying in the context of a more public occasion, for we, as readers, also re-enact the ritual—the awareness of this death and the placing of it within the larger context of human experience. The ceremonial takes both poet and reader far beyond death itself. The possibility of artistic transcendence is affirmed and celebrated, and the reader participates in that transcendence through his experience with the poem itself.[4]

Herrick's other burial instructions, of which there are a surprisingly large number, deviate in smaller points from the form of "To Perilla," but all attempt to come to grips with and to go beyond the same natural end. More in keeping with our specifically pastoral expectations is "To Laurels" (H-89):

4. Cf. Deming's assertion that the ritual of mourning does not transcend death or eternalize the individual, but simply provides the proper and fitting conclusion to the act of dying ("The Classical Ceremonial," pp. 108–9, 225). Deming here seems to confuse ritual as poetic device with ritual as literal action, but even if the rite were literal, it is by definition periodically re-enacted by the mourners—just as it is poetically re-enacted by the readers of the poem. In each instance, the rite serves as an eternalizing agent by continually reinvoking remembrance of the individual whom it celebrates.

> A Funerall stone,
>   Or Verse I covet none;
>   But only crave
>   Of you, that I may have
> A sacred Laurel springing from my grave:
>   Which being seen,
>   Blest with perpetuall greene,
>   May grow to be
>   Not so much call'd a tree,
> As the eternall monument of me.

The poem is representative of a series in which the instructing or pleading speaker addresses laurels, yews, cypress, and other trees and flowers. The plea is always the same: that the continuous growth of the natural object will serve as a living memorial to him. In this poem, he first addresses the laurel as a "sacred" plant, "springing" from his grave. The choice of "springing" evokes associations of the season —growth, freshness, vitality—all of which are appropriate to the plea. The religious connotations of "sacred" are reemphasized as the plant is next seen "Blest" with "perpetuall greene." The evergreen quality extends the image of spring in time and helps to define the laurel's "sacred" nature. Also significant is the emphatic "of me" in the final line, the explicit connection between the speaker himself and the natural object. The ever-green and ever-springing laurel becomes the speaker as nature itself provides a means of negating death.

"His embalming to Julia" (H-327) represents a more specialized form of burial instruction:

> FOr my embalming, *Julia*, do but this,
> Give thou my lips but their supreamest kiss:
> Or else trans-fuse thy breath into the chest,
> Where my small reliques must for ever rest:
> That breath the *Balm*, the *myrrh*, the *Nard* shal be,
> To give an *incorruption* unto me.

Ostensibly, the poem is a request for "incorruption," for forestalling the "putrefying" end of the death-process. The agent of the embalming is Julia; the means, her breath. The poem is effective, especially in the pun on "supreamest," which here probably carries the meaning of "last, final, as belonging to the moment of death" (*OED*), in addition to the more common adjectival sense of "highest" or "best." But the emphasis in the poem is not on any transcendence for the speaker, but rather on Julia herself. In providing Julia with religious significance, the poem becomes an elaborate verse-compliment instead of the kind of artistic transcendence described above.

"To Julia" (H-499) takes the opening lines of this poem and transforms them into a new and different statement:

> *JUlia*, when thy *Herrick* dies,
> Close thou up thy Poets eyes:
> And his last breath, let it be
> Taken in by none but Thee.

The ceremony here is severely limited and simplified, but as is usual with Herrick that very act of simplification accomplishes a forceful emotional impact. Nonetheless, though the poem is a masterful compression of feeling and an explanation or at least a suggestion of just how much is involved in the "supreamest kiss," it does not take the speaker very far beyond the finality of death. The ceremony merely transforms the act of dying into an intense and devotional union of the two lovers.

The ceremonial treatment in "To his lovely Mistresses" (H-634) is much closer to that in "To Perilla":

> ONe night i'th'yeare, my dearest Beauties, come
> And bring those *dew-drink-offerings* to my Tomb.
> When thence ye see my reverend Ghost to rise,
> And there to lick th'effused sacrifice:
> Though palenes be the Livery that I weare,
> Looke ye not wan, or colourlesse for feare.
> Trust me I will not hurt ye; or once shew
> The least grim looke, or cast a frown on you:
> Nor shall the Tapers when I'm there, burn blew.
> This I may do (perhaps) as I glide by,

> Cast on my Girles a glance, and loving eye:
> Or fold mine armes, and sigh, because I've lost
> The world so soon, and in it, you the most.
> Then these, no feares more on your Fancies fall,
> Though then I smile, and speake no words at all.

Literally, the poem contains the ritual of mourning which Herrick
continually uses in similar instructions and which provides a "yeerly"
transcendence of death's finality through the memorial nature of the
rites. In addition to the element of a fairly light-hearted Cavalier
humor obvious on one level of the poem's meaning, the fanciful depiction of the ghost rising to accept the offered effusions provides Herrick
with a means of demonstrating the significance of the ritual by emphasizing the speaker's serenity. The delicate control of emotional
tone here is one of the real achievements of the poem, an achievement
made possible chiefly by the ceremonial form. The artistic stasis allows
the speaker's death to be continuously commemorated ritualistically,
and his response to that ritual indicates its value. Most important in
this response is his concern not to frighten those participating in the
rite. This unexpected, and somewhat humorous, redirection of emotional concern convinces the reader that the ceremony is effective. The
final line, "Though then I smile, and speake no words at all," is a
highly compressed statement in which the speaker's emotion is perfectly controlled, yielding a sense of utter serenity. The ceremonial
takes reader and speaker far beyond death itself, for death, at the end
of this poem, is simply irrelevant.

"Upon himselfe being buried" (H-549) shows a totally different
concern:

> LEt me sleep this night away,
> Till the Dawning of the day:
> Then at th'opening of mine eyes,
> I, and all the world shall rise.

The equating of death and sleep (including, of course, the allusion to
the Last Judgment and the awakening of all the dead) is traditional

in Christian poetry and the image is reminiscent of Donne's "Death be not proud":

> One short sleep past, we wake eternally,
> And death shall be no more: death, thou shalt die.
>
> (ll. 13–14)

This particular means of transcending death is not often invoked in the *Hesperides*, and when it is Herrick opens himself to the kinds of dangers noted with the Christian epigrams. In the burial poems, however, he manages to avoid the stock formulae and, in fact, frequently achieves some of his most impressive poetic statements in this vein. Part of the reason for his success in these particular poems is that he can count on a wider range of compacted emotions because of the reader's probable familiarity with the concepts—he can, that is, concentrate on the manipulation of feelings rather than the development of a possible transcendence since the latter is already assumed.

All the poems examined thus far are artistic ceremonials, for the transcendence achieved is primarily a *poetic* one: it is outside the realm of actual fact and is accomplished by a specifically artistic creation. Herrick's affective intent in these poems can be defined in similar terms: he invites the reader to affirm the possibility of artistic transcendence and to participate in it by experiencing the poem itself. These burial instructions are concerned mainly with establishing a realm of poetic stasis in which the act of death becomes somehow more significant than its natural or actual fact would warrant. The poems are not really an attempt to escape the reality of death, but an artistic placing of the natural act within a more meaningful and less "final" context of human experience.

The epitaph is the second pastoral form included in the artistic ceremonial. It is perhaps a deliberate counterpart to the burial instruction, for it often seeks to evoke in the reader the same responses of recognition, pity, and commemoration (often, in fact, in the same ritualistic terms), while at the same time making the plea for those responses even more public and universal. On the whole, though, the attempt to transcend death is conducted here along somewhat different lines. For one thing, the epitaph is a more conventional "poetic" ceremony. Although it has not been noted as often or as emphatically as necessary, the epitaph, like the ode or the elegy, is one of the traditional poetic forms through which the poet-mourner can confront the fact of death and achieve some measure of consolation.[5] Frequently such consolation comes by way of the epitaph's memorial inscription, for in presenting the essence of the dead person the poet actually recreates the character of that individual in a more static and permanent form.[6] Herrick's artistry in this particular form is most often revealed, however, not in the precision of his portraits, but in the subtle manipulation of the reader's emotional response to the death, a response which is simultaneously purgative, cognitive, and ceremonial. That is, Herrick takes the reader from feelings of sorrow, anxiety, and instability at the opening of the poem to ones of peace and serenity at the close; he redirects attention from the deceased individual to the reader himself, creating in the latter an awareness of the significance of this death to him personally;[7] and he always takes the reader beyond mourning to a rite of celebration. All the epitaphs of the *Hesperides* attempt to place death in a framework of emotional implications which provide it with more meaning and importance than it would otherwise have. Poet and reader are ceremonially united with the deceased in a static moment of celebration in which the literal death often becomes irrelevant.

5. Like all burial poems, the epitaph usually contains three clearly defined sections: the *epainos*, or ceremonial praise of the individual; the *threnos*, or song of lament; and the *paramuthia*, or consolation. Hence, all epitaphs provide the poet with a ready-made progression from dejection to consolation and resolution. See O. B. Hardison, Jr., *The Enduring Monument* (Chapel Hill, 1962), pp. 113–15.

6. Cf. Smith's assertion, noted earlier, that the epigram (she includes the epitaph in this genre) "seems to be the last word on its subject. . . . whatever an inscription was wanted to identify or characterize something both briefly and permanently, the epigram would stand, for all time, to all readers, as the ultimately appropriate statement thereupon" (*Poetic Closure*, p. 196).

7. Rollin, discussing the child-epitaphs to be examined shortly, comes close to describing this cognitive feature: "The death of a child is not only a deprivation of the parents; it is an event which diminishes all of us. And it poignantly reawakens our awareness of the brevity of human existence, an existence of which we are, as the child once was, a part" (*Robert Herrick*, p. 35).

"Upon the much lamented, Master J. Warr" (H-134) is an example of the traditional epitaph form:

> WHat Wisdome, Learning, Wit, or Worth,
> Youth, or sweet Nature, co'd bring forth,
> Rests here with him; who was the Fame,
> The Volumne of himselfe, and Name.
> If, Reader, then thou wilt draw neere,
> And doe an honour to thy teare;
> Weep then for him, for whom laments
> Not one, but many Monuments.[8]

The poem is divided conventionally into two equal parts: lines 1–4 present a *summary description* of Warr himself, and lines 5–8 present an *exhortation* to the reader, directing him to the proper emotional response. The summary description is typical enough: the speaker chooses some representative virtues (usually wisdom, learning, wit, courage, or prowess for a man; beauty, faith, love, or chastity for a woman) which found their natural incarnation in this man and which are now extinct because their earthly form is dead.

The exhortation is somewhat less conventional, for instead of simply directing the reader to show his capacity for pity by weeping over this lamentable death, the speaker inverts the beneficiary. The reader's tear does not honor Warr as much as Warr's death honors his tear: "And doe an honour to thy teare." Warr's death, that is, and the

---

8. McEuen suggests (in *Classical Influence upon the Tribe of Ben,* p. 238) that the poem owes something to the following anonymous Greek epigram:

> The tomb possesses Paterius, sweet-spoken and loveable, the dear son of Miltiades and sorrowing Atticia, a child of Athens of the noble race of Aeacidae, full of knowledge of Roman law and of all wisdom, endowed with the brilliance of all the four virtues, a young man of charm, whom Fate carried off, even as the whirlwind uproots a beautiful sapling. He was in his twenty-fourth year and left to his dear parents undying lament and mourning.

But the whole conception of Paterius is different from Herrick's of Warr: Paterius is simply a virtuous youth; Warr is the "issue" of the Virtues. In addition, the epigram contains nothing like Herrick's last four lines. The two poems are so different in form and treatment that McEuen's connection of the two seems wholly groundless.

reader's response to that death, are equally important and interdependent—both allow a demonstration of essential humanity. This is not sentimentality, at least not in any derogatory sense, but an expression of feeling for, and a recognition of oneness with, another human being. Furthermore, Herrick's redirecting of the reader's response is at the center of the ceremonial, because the poem provides the reader with a ritualistic and formal act which, if he participates, makes this death more significant than merely the end of a person's life. The rite makes the poem a vehicle for a ceremonial union of one being with another. By showing his feeling for Warr, the reader is united with him in a static moment in which the literal death is of no account.

A similar use of the epitaph appears in "Upon a comely, and curious Maide" (H-564):

> IF Men can say that beauty dyes;
> Marbles will sweare that here it lyes.
> If Reader then thou canst forbeare,
> In publique loss to shed a Teare:
> The Dew of griefe upon this stone
> Will tell thee *Pitie* thou hast none.

By shortening the summary description to just two lines, Herrick focuses attention on the exhortation, which is here more vehement than that in the preceding poem. Actually, it inverts the previous injunction: if the reader does not weep, he will disclose (and discover) his heartlessness and callousness. Once again the emphasis is on the reader's response, not on the person who has died; the death is given additional significance because it provides a means toward self-awareness and emotional commitment. Also important is the fact that this death is a "publique loss." All Herrick's epitaphs seek to convince the reader that such is the case, for only if he is related to the death can he respond emotionally to it and participate in the ceremonial union the artist and the poem demand.

In "Upon a Maide" (H-838) Herrick combines the conventional summary description of the epitaph with the ritual of mourning of the burial instruction:

> HEre she lyes (in Bed of Spice)
> Faire as *Eve* in Paradice:
> For her beauty it was such
> Poets co'd not praise too much.
> Virgins Come, and in a Ring
> Her supreamest *Requiem* sing;
> Then depart, but see ye tread
> Lightly, lightly ore the dead.

The final lines still concentrate on the emotional response to this death, but they add an element of sacramental ritual to heighten the importance of that response. The last line is a good indication of the poet's emotional control as the simple repetition of the word "lightly" provides a feeling of tender and ritualistic concern appropriate to this "supreamest *Requiem*."[9] And, of course, "supreamest" may again carry the punning connotations already seen in "His embalming to Julia."

Two more short poems dealing with this combination of epitaph description and burial mourning are "An Epitaph upon a child" (H-125) and "Upon a Child. An Epitaph" (H-180):

> VIrgins promis'd when I dy'd,
> That they wo'd each Primrose-tide,
> Duely, Morne and Ev'ning, come,
> And with flowers dresse my Tomb.
> Having promis'd, pay your debts,
> Maids, and here strew Violets.

> *   *   *

> BUt borne, and like a short Delight,
> I glided by my Parents sight.
> That done, the harder Fates deny'd
> My longer stay, and so I dy'd.

9. Herrick uses the words "lightly" or "lightly tread" as a closing injunction in several epitaphs. It is an emotional adaptation of a conventional classical ending: *Sit tibi perpetuo terra levis tumulo* (cf. Martial, *Epigrammata* V.xxxiv.9–10).

> If pittying my sad Parents Teares,
> You'l spil a tear, or two with theirs:
> And with some flowers my grave bestrew,
> Love and they'l thank you for't. Adieu.

The first poem presents a typical plea for the burial instruction's ritual of mourning and remembrance, and emphasizes two aspects of that rite: its repetitiveness ("each Primrose-tide," "Duely, Morne and Ev'ning") and its fulfillment by means of rather simple yet sanctifying acts (here strewing violets). The second poem is formally closer to those constructed of summary description and exhortation. The description gives an important emphasis to the poem by defining the child in terms of the parents. The image of line 2, the child's "gliding" by her parents' sight, is effective in capturing the fleeting nature of time (and hence life), and is reminiscent of one of Herrick's epigrams:

> THousands each day passe by, which wee,
> Once past and gone, no more shall see.
>
> (H-671)

Furthermore, by focusing attention on the parents' sight, the image prepares for and supports the redirection of emotion in the exhortation, not toward the child herself, but toward those parents. It is a peculiar twist, although, as the final line clarifies in its emphasis on "love," the end of the emotional appeal is still the same—ceremonial oneness and cognition of human feeling. In a sense, the reader is asked to become the parent of this child.

These little epitaphs on children are among Herrick's best in the genre. In them he rings some of his finest emotional tones, all within the very limited space afforded by the form. To illustrate, we may examine two child-epitaphs which are, on the surface, almost identical. The first is "Upon a child that dyed" (H-310):

> HEre she lies, a pretty bud,
> Lately made of flesh and blood:
> Who, as soone, fell fast asleep,
> As her little eyes did peep.

> Give her strewings; but not stir
> The earth, that lightly covers her.

The poem begins by equating the child with a tender and fragile bud, then personifies this image by adding "flesh and blood." The next two lines advance the summary description by giving the process of her death. Her "peeping" eyes might be intended to carry on the "bud" image of line 1, in which case the bud would be just breaking through its calyx—only to be covered up again. And the poem ends with the traditional Roman exhortation to give strewings and not to disturb the grave.

The epitaph is serious, somber, and delicate; it presents an appropriately tender image for the child; it has a consistent and logical three-part movement; and it evokes the intended emotions of reverence, pity, sorrow, and so forth. Further, by directing attention away from the literal death to the figure of the child herself, Herrick has constructed a poetic ritual in which the reader is united with him in an act of ceremonial commemoration. That the child has died is finally not as important as the fact that her death provides a means of celebrating her. She becomes, in a sense, more important than she was because of the artistic ritual her death occasions. Nonetheless, the poem is not totally satisfactory, for the statement seems too emaciated, the major image serves no developing function, and emotional response is not directed and controlled carefully enough.

In what is surely a later version[10] of the same poem, "Upon a child" (H-640), Herrick adds considerable life to the death-portrait:

> HEre a pretty Baby lies
> Sung asleep with Lullabies:
> Pray be silent, and not stirre
> Th'easie earth that covers her.

10. There is, of course, no sure way of dating these poems and position in the volume cannot be trusted to mirror chronology; still, what evidence we do have concerning Herrick's revisions suggests that economy was one of his guiding principles and this makes it probable that "Upon a child" is the later of the two poems.

The poem's title is ambiguous and does not immediately limit the work to the epitaph genre, although that possibility is not excluded either. The significance of the ambiguity is appreciated when we see that it is only in the final line that we learn for sure that the child is dead. Thus Herrick can develop certain emotional attitudes and elicit certain responses unencumbered by the austere fact of the child's death.

The opening line, "HEre a pretty Baby lies," presents the literal image of a child asleep on a bed or in a crib and evokes feelings of tenderness, peace, and security. The second line reinforces this image and these emotions, but takes them a step farther. The reference to singing the child asleep with "Lullabies" evokes emotional associations of maternity, thereby adding feelings of love and concern to those established by line 1. This is a conventional summary description and the first half of the poem ends. But the description is conventional only in the structural sense, for nothing has yet been said about the child herself—attention is focused strictly on the emotional context in which the child is seen. And, to repeat, neither the subject matter of the couplet nor the tense of its verbs gives any sure indication that the baby is dead. We seem to be in a suspended present.

With line 3, "Pray be silent, and not stirre," the exhortation begins. Literally, the line implies that if the reader is not silent, or if he stirs, the child will awaken. Though a new section of the poem has begun, the image and emotional overtones of the first part are carried on. But there is one important change simply by virtue of the imperative: the reader is drawn into this tender, peaceful setting, made an actual participant, and given the responsibility to maintain the scene exactly as he found it.

In the final line the child's death is bluntly confronted. Although this death was never quite beyond expectation, the depiction of the intensely emotional situation makes the suddenly factual emphasis somewhat startling. The literal image immediately alters: the earth itself is both bed and blankets. Yet the change in image is not really that drastic, for the visual picture is not one of a grave either. The insertion of the word "earth" in that part of the final line where we expect to find "covers," and the use of "covers" to define the action of the earth rather than as a noun describing the baby's blankets, maintain the identical image of the first three lines. Only the "material" of the bed has changed. Similarly, though the knowledge of the child's death is now certain, the emotional attitudes and responses are not significantly altered either. They may be deepened by a gentle poignancy, but peace, calm, serenity, and love are still the dominant tones.

If the image and emotional responses remain the same, what of the exhortation? It seems clear that it too is unchanged by virtue of the description of the earth as "easie." Of course, "easie" could refer to the fact that the grave is freshly dug, but that places too realistic an emphasis on the actual and jars with image and tone at this point. Even the more conventional sense of "not pressing tightly" seems inappropriate at this point. More likely is the implication that the earth is "easie" just as a child's blanket would be "easie": if, as the exhortation warns, *either* is disturbed, whether by noise or movement, the child will awaken. The assumption behind the line is not that death is analogous to sleep, but that death is sleep. The child will quite literally awaken when this "easie" earth is stirred. There is nothing especially unique about the idea itself, particularly for an Anglican priest. In the vision of the Valley of Dry Bones in Ezekiel, the Spirit of God says, "O my people, I will open your graves, and cause you to come up out of your graves . . ."; according to Matthew 27:52, at the ninth hour of the crucifixion, "the graves were opened, and many bodies of the saints which slept, arose . . ."; and Jesus, according to John 5:28–29, says that "the hour is coming in which all that are in the graves shall hear his [the Son's] voice, and shall come forth. . . ." Herrick uses similar Christian associations with the word "sleep" in "To the Lady Crew, upon the death of her Child" (H-514), "On himselfe" (H-306), "His own Epitaph" (H-617), "Upon his kinswoman Mistris Elizabeth Herrick" (H-376), and "Upon himselfe being buried" (H-549). What is unique is his revitalization here of the stock classical ending of "Upon a child that dyed" for an effective consolation.

By presenting a carefully controlled action involving the speaker, the child, and the reader, the epitaph becomes its own poetic ritual;

and that rite, by enlisting the reader's participation and by directing his emotional response, transforms the literal death into a transcendent sleep, a waiting for the Last Judgment. More than the earlier version, the poem exploits the ceremonial possibilities: it asks, indeed demands, celebration and commemoration rather than mourning. The control of image and emotional tone here demonstrates Herrick's poetic ceremonial at its very best. The reader is taken with the poet into a controlled artistic stasis in which death as an inevitable natural fact becomes suddenly quite irrelevant.

The control that the ceremonial nature of Herrick's epitaphs exerts over the emotional context can be seen in one final example, "An Epitaph upon a Virgin" (H-450):

> HEre a solemne Fast we keepe,
> While all beauty lyes asleep
> Husht be all things; (no noyse here)
> But the toning of a teare:
> Or a sigh of such as bring
> Cowslips for her covering.

The rite here is similar to that in previous poems, but the emotional force of that rite is underscored by the poet's subtle use of alliteration in the final three lines, as well as by the sensitive and intensely felt image of "the toning of a teare." The serenity evoked in "Upon a child" is again called forth here, this time more by language than by association. And again the tone, the mood, and the ceremonial governing both extend the significance of the death far beyond its natural "end."

The importance of Herrick's burial instructions and epitaphs to the volume as a whole cannot be overemphasized. The sheer number of them suggests that the poet is somehow deeply committed to the ceremonial artistry they portray. The key to this art is the ceremonial's power to transform death into an act or state of more meaning, more public and universal significance, than its literal condition would warrant. Death is transcended, though not escaped, by means of a *poetic* rite: the speaker and the reader are transported from the graveyard to a heightened, controlled, and ordered stasis of art itself.

In "A Dirge upon the Death of the Right Valiant Lord, Bernard Stuart" (H-219), Herrick combines both the memorializing summary of the epitaph and the ritual of mourning of the burial instruction. More important, however, is his use of both pastoral means of transcendence to prepare for a third means—the promise of *poetic* immortality.

    1. HEnce, hence, profane; soft silence let us have;
       While we this *Trentall* sing about thy Grave.

    2. Had Wolves or Tigers seen but thee,
       They wo'd have shew'd civility;
       And in compassion of thy yeeres,
       Washt those thy purple wounds with tears.
       But since th'art slaine; and in thy fall,
       The drooping Kingdome suffers all.

Chorus

This we will doe; we'll daily come
And offer Tears upon thy Tomb:
And if that they will not suffice,
Thou shalt have soules for sacrifice.

Sleepe in thy peace, while we with spice perfume thee,
And *Cedar* wash thee, that no times consume thee.

    3. Live, live thou dost, and shalt; for why?
       Soules doe not with their bodies die:
       Ignoble off-springs, they may fall
       Into the flames of Funerall:
       When as the chosen seed shall spring
       Fresh, and for ever flourishing.

Chorus

And times to come shall, weeping, read thy glory,
Lesse in these Marble stones, then in thy story.

The poem begins with a two-line invocation, or, more specifically, a call to the ritual of mourning. The "*Trentall*," of course, as a dirge, refers to the poem itself; in a like manner, the ceremonial of the described rites is also the ceremonial of art—here the construction of a complete masquelike ritual in which the reader is asked to participate.

Lines 3–8 present a summary description, though one a bit different from the preceding mainly because of the kinds of allusions made. The first of these, the "Wolves or Tigers" which "wo'd have shew'd [Stuart] civility," refers to the depiction in Genesis of man living in accord with all the animals. Stuart becomes therefore the noble and unfallen Adam, the archetypal man-figure. The next allusion carries this elevation even further, for line 6, by referring to the "purple wounds" washed with tears, alludes to and associates Stuart with Christ, the *novus* Adam, in whose death (literally, not allegorically) "the drooping Kingdome suffers all." It is not necessary to suggest any archetypal myths at work in the poem, although the need to overcome the fact of death by constructing "singing monuments" does have mythic proportion. This point is simply that the character of Stuart is elevated to almost supernatural status by the allusions. This is not a typical summary description, even though most are rhetorically inflated.

The chorus responds to this description by reinvoking the same ritual of commemoration seen in other burial poems. By anointing the body in order to preserve it from the "end" of "putrefaction," the chorus emphasizes that the concern for stasis, even now that Stuart is dead, is still paramount.

At line 15 the focus shifts as attention is directed not so much to the present or past Stuart as to his "future." The lines provide a specifically Christian hope based upon a set of natural images. The key to those images occurs in the final two lines of the section:

> When as the chosen seed shall spring
> Fresh, and for ever flourishing.

"Seed," "spring," "fresh," and "flourishing" all evoke associations of the natural regenerative cycle, but these associations are placed within a Christian supernatural context by line 16: "*Soules doe not with their bodies die.*" "Chosen" calls to mind once again the Adamic motif by making Stuart one of his lineage.

Again the chorus responds, although the response is quite different. Stuart's glory will be remembered not by the lines on his tombstone or by their rituals, or even by his Christian immortality, but by his "story." As we will discover from Herrick's other artistic ceremonials, his use of "story" here refers to poetry. It is this poem, in fact, which preserves Stuart and insures his immortality by seeing to it that "no times consume" him. All means of transcendence are ultimately subsumed under and find their resolution in the artistic ceremonial itself and for that reason the concluding lines of the "Dirge" are appropriate. Art provides for, gives reality to, and is less qualified than all the other separate means of transcendence, for only art is finally and visually successful in creating a stasis outside time.

ii. THE COURTLY VOICE

To jump from the pastoral burial poems to the courtly poems of the present section requires a measure of readjustment. For one thing, the courtly persona, at least in the first group of poems to be discussed, is far less willing than his pastoral counterpart to dwell at length on death itself. Instead, he generally seeks a means of forestalling even the mention of death by constructing specific courtly ceremonies, very similar at times to those outlined in Chapter III. The difference between the ones in that chapter and those to be treated here is that the ceremonial of the present group is a more strictly poetic one, not a literal action. For this reason, the precise working out of the ceremonial form is often quite distinctive.

The courtly poems which fall into this context of the artistic ceremonial can be divided into two categories, the Bacchanalian and the dedicatory. The former class is concerned with establishing a way of life that will give total emphasis to the present and in this way negate the forces of mutability and death, at least for the duration of the rite it constructs. Most of these poems imitate classical poets, frequently

Anacreon. Consequently, Herrick here emphasizes the *carpe diem* motif in frolicsome, even "lusty," terms. In a more historical light, these lyrics attempt to capture and reinvoke all that we have learned to associate with the "Sons of Ben"—the Devil's Tavern, and Apollo Room, the drinking and carousing, the spirited recitation of and discussions about poetry, the closely knit fellowship, the lively and goodnatured frolic implicit in such poems as "Ben. Jonsons Sociable Rules for the Apollo." In short, the speaker here is the sportive reveler known among his compatriots as "The musick of a Feast."

"A Lyrick to Mirth" (H-111) is a perfect capsule summary of the atmosphere of these particular "Tribe" songs:

> WHile the milder Fates consent,
> Let's enjoy our merryment:
> Drink, and dance, and pipe, and play;
> Kisse our *Dollies* night and day:
> Crown'd with clusters of the Vine;
> Let us sit, and quaffe our wine.
> Call on *Bacchus*; chaunt his praise;
> Shake the *Thyrse*, and bite the *Bayes*:
> Rouze *Anacreon* from the dead;
> And return him drunk to bed:
> Sing o're *Horace*; for ere long
> Death will come and mar the song:
> Then shall *Wilson* and *Gotiere*
> Never sing, or play more here.

The poem "sings" a specific kind of celebratory activity, identified in the title as "mirth" and in the second line as "merryment." The essential purpose of the work is to present an invitation to join in the activity. More consciously than in the poems of the courtly persona examined earlier, the speaker here provides the pressing reasons for participation. Not only does this feature give an additional sense of urgency to the appeal, but, as seen in poems like "Corinna," forces the reader to accept, celebrate, and take part in the action to which the poet invites him.

Although the poem is fairly short, there is a progressive development and there are four distinct sections. The first (ll. 1–2) and fourth (ll. 11–14) present the context in which the experience is to be viewed; two and three (ll. 3–6; 7–10) detail the activity itself. The opening section not only defines the kind of experience to follow ("merryment"), but sets precise limits on that experience. Every word of the first line is important in terms of the restrictions. "While," of course, implies both a suspension of time and a knowledge that the suspension will be, at best, only a brief instant. The "milder Fates" are obviously Clotho and Lachesis, those "sisters" concerned with the *life* of man. The allusion is functional in recalling another, less "mild" Fate (Atropos) and in preparing for her emergence in the twelfth line of the poem. And "consent" implies that man has little control over his own life, for even the "milder" Fates, by assigning life and lots (stations on the hierarchical Chain of Being), affect that life more profoundly than man himself. A rather serious and ominous opening for a lyric to "mirth."

In the next four lines (3–6) Herrick enters the activity of "merryment" and provides the first details as to just what it includes. "Drink, and dance, and pipe, and play" are specific festive acts and evoke exactly the opposite emotional response from that invoked by the first line. Here is a pure courtly sportiveness, which is nicely capped off by the Bacchanalian references to "clusters of vine" and the quaffing of wine. There is a sense of free, unrestricted, almost wanton giving in to the festive spirit in these lines, a freedom which is deliberately contrasted with the lack of choice in the first two lines and toward which the reader is asked to respond affirmatively. In the next quatrain (7–10) some order is reimposed upon the activity, though not enough to limit unrestrained "merryment." Bacchus and Anacreon, conventional figures of drink and sport, are called upon for their authoritarian approval. The *"Thyrse"* and *"Bayes"* (according to Herrick's typical usage) allude to poetry and prepare for the appearance, in the eleventh line, of Horace, the arch-poet.

The final section of the poem (11–14), then, begins with this appearance. Horace has every right to be here, of course, because his *carpe diem* injunction is the foundation of the plea made in the middle eight lines. It is significant, therefore, that his name is linked not with the sportive rites but with the entrance of death. Horace, perhaps more than any of the classical authors, emphasized the *carpe diem* philosophy as a serious response to the inevitable "end" of death; [11] Herrick, more than most English Horatian disciples, follows this emphasis rigorously. Atropos has arrived and the poem ends where it began, with the clear insistence that "Death will come and mar the song," that we shall "Never sing, or play more here." This acknowledgment makes even more necessary a commitment to the kind of activity outlined in the second and third sections. Death will not be put off, but it can at least be put out of mind.

Looking again at the overall pattern of the poem, it is clear that the first and fourth sections provide a context within which the activity of sections two and three is both justified and necessitated. In other words, sections two and three are poetic moments of suspended time, a ritual of festivity, created, heightened, and concluded because of the actuality and inevitability of the death surrounding them in sections one and four. As noted earlier, it is mainly in terms of the artistic ceremonial that the message has its most forceful impact, for even in the poem itself, where time theoretically can be suspended indefinitely, that suspension lasts for only eight short lines. Recognition of this fact demands immediate affirmation of the significance of the middle festival, but also emphasizes its most important qualification: it only suspends time; it does not stop it. As frequently happens in the pastoral and courtly poems examined in the earlier chapters, Herrick's insistence on the limits of his artistic rite not only demonstrates a serious concern with that ritual, but seriously weakens the affirmation and celebration to which the reader is invited. Poetry can, the lyric seems to say, carry us into a unique realm of ritualistic festivity in which the thought of mutability is momentarily obliterated; but it

---

11. See Frederick Henry Candelaria, "The *Carpe Diem* Motif in Early Seventeenth-Century Lyric Poetry with Particular Reference to Robert Herrick," diss., Univ. of Missouri, 1959, p. 50, as well as his discussion of the relationship between this motif and the *ubi sunt* and *sic transit gloria mundi* themes (pp. 54ff).

cannot keep us in that realm for very long as reality swiftly reclaims us.

"A Frolick" (H-582) and "Anacreontike" (H-540) represent two more approaches to the kind of festivity outlined in "A Lyric to Mirth":

> BRing me my Rose-buds, Drawer come;
>   So, while I thus sit crown'd;
> Ile drink the aged *Cecubum*,
>   Untill the roofe turne round.

*   *   *

> BOrn I was to be old,
>   And for to die here:
> After that, in the mould
>   Long for to lye here.
> But before that day comes,
>   Still I be Bousing;
> For I know, in the Tombs
>   There's no Carousing.

As in several of the other Bacchanalian verses, "A Frolick" begins directly with the rite of "merryment" and remains there for the duration of the poem. The reader's participation in that rite, however, is enlisted only by the freedom of the speaker's own emotional attitude, by his abandonment. Because the reader is not given enough evidence to affirm actively the importance of what the speaker is doing, he cannot recognize the full import of the festivity. "Anacreontike" shows the opposite extreme, for the speaker here defines the realistic context without much or enough ceremony. The first four lines describe the inevitable end of earthly existence and the final four give the *carpe diem* answer—"Bousing." But the "Bousing" takes only two short lines and the poem ends on a Marvellian note of death once more without having constructed any rite per se. Neither poem is as artistically successful as "A Lyric to Mirth."

The most famous of the Bacchanalian poems is "The Welcome to

Sack" (H-197). Although the poem is frequently anthologized, critical commentary on it is relatively sparse. It is a remarkable work, however, from several different angles (one of which is its relation to the companion piece, "His fare-well to Sack" [H-128]) and needs a more careful reading. The "Welcome" is an extended love poem displaying all the rhetorical flights, elaborate compliments, and passionate fervor of an Elizabethan sonnet. By substituting wine for the mistress, Herrick is able to effect a great deal of irony and parody which make the poem a tour de force, or, in more appropriate seventeenth-century language, a paradoxical encomium. It can be divided into five sections: invocation and welcome (ll. 1–18), questions on past absence (ll. 19–48), protestation of mistress's (wine's) power to "move" (ll. 49–68), the invitation (ll. 69–80), and the vow of eternal constancy (ll. 81–92).

The opening section of the poem presents four extended analogies. The first two, equating the merging of two streams with the uniting of two lovers, serve to define the emotional attitude of the persona as joyful, desirous, anxious, and relieved. The scarcity of this kind of extended simile in Herrick's verse argues a special and deliberate rhetorical treatment here. The third analogy equates Sack with the "Eternall Lamp of Love," whose beams are brighter than the sun. This analogy, with its emphasis on Sack's ability to "out-glare" and "out-shine," is an obvious parody of the verse-compliment, for if the eyes of the conventional Elizabethan and Cavalier mistress are not shooting darts of love, they are "out-shining" something or other, usually the sun. The fourth analogy relates the joy of Ulysses' homecoming to the speaker's reunion with Sack. Much of the irony of this particular image, as well as many others in the poem, depends upon the knowledge that the speaker had bid Sack farewell only a few (70) poems earlier.

The function of all these analogies is to establish the tone and identity of the speaker. He is a lover who can see his beloved only in inflated and elaborate terms; he is so emotionally overcome that he must translate his feelings into hyperbolic similes. But although the opening situation is a parody of the typical Petrarchan love-malady, there is no indication of moral censure or disparagement. The irony (in the incongruity between a mistress and Sack) and the parody simply add to the lighthearted play and humor of the poem. At the same time, casting Sack in the role of a mistress is a means of magnifying (though perhaps not seriously) the wine itself and this, of course, beyond the more elemental playing with conventions, is the intention of a paradoxical encomium.

The second section of the poem is again a deliberate parody of the typical lover's condition. Here the speaker pleads with the mistress-wine and demands an answer for her previous absence. He questions her general motives, whether or not her absence was caused by some fault of his own, and finally confesses that actually he left her (as we know from the "Fare-well")—not because he loathed her, but to "enflame" his "zeale." The section ends with a capsule summary of the "impossibilities" motif:

> ... thy Iles shall lack
> Grapes, before *Herrick* leaves Canarie Sack.
>
> (ll. 47–48)

The third section of the poem is concerned with the power and influence of Sack. Nothing could make the lover as "ayrie" or "nimble" or more inspired than she. It is incredible that the Egyptians and Cassius did not recognize this power; after all, both Cato and Hercules attest to it. Sack becomes even more apotheosized by the added weight of classical authority. The speaker now feels free to invite the "sanctified" mistress-wine to join with him, for "Love and lust," in a Bacchanalian ravishment:

> Swell up my nerves with spirit; let my blood
> Run through my veines, like to a hasty flood.
> Fill each part full of fire, active to doe
> What thy commanding soule shall put it to.
>
> (ll. 77–80)

The poem seemingly ends with a protestation of faithfulness and a plea by the lover that he be damned in various ways ("Call me *The*

sonne of Beere, and then confine/ Me to the Tap, the Tost, the Turfe
. . .") if he should break his oath. The last five lines, though, shift
the whole focus of the poem:

> . . . Let Wine
> Ne'er shine upon me; May my Numbers all
> Run to a sudden Death, and Funerall.
> And last, when thee (deare Spouse) I disavow,
> Ne'r may Prophetique *Daphne* crown my Brow.
>
> (ll. 88–92)

The emphasis here is not on Sack at all, but on poetry and on the
assumption that the inspiration for that verse will prevent it from
dying, will win for it the eternity of the laurel crown. There is a
suspicion at the end that underlying the parody and the elaborately
contrived irony of the poem may be something more serious. Whereas
the mistress of the poem is actually Sack, Sack itself may be a metaphor
for poetic inspiration. The poem therefore may be a plea for and a
demonstration of an artistic power strong enough and active enough
to keep fate in check (l. 71) and to keep death from claiming it.

The poem is still (perhaps even primarily) an exercise in poetic
wit, but such a reading, though obvious enough, depends upon a fuller
comparison with some typical Elizabethan love lyrics. Nonetheless,
the poem can also be seen as a ceremonial in the same form as "A
Lyrick to Mirth." It presents an elevated and meaningful stasis in
which the Bacchanalian commitment to experience demands celebration of and participation in the festive spirit of mirth and merriment.
The poem demonstrates the truth of what it says: wine, as a poetic
subject, has the power to move the poet to create a lasting and significant work of art, and for that reason alone justly merits praise and
apotheosis.

Two final Bacchanalian ceremonials can be mentioned here—
"When he would have his verses read" (H-8) and "To live merrily,
and to trust to Good Verses" (H-201). Because the first poem is so
important in terms of the conceptions Herrick's artistic persona holds
about his craft, discussion of it must be postponed momentarily. "To

live merrily" is a working out of the "influence" that the speaker claims Sack has on him in the "Welcome." The poem begins with three stanzas describing the setting: it is spring, a time of festivity and celebration; the "golden Pomp" has returned to the earth and "Now raignes the Rose" (a key line in "When he would have his verses read" also). The Bacchanalian persona, not to be omitted from this natural revitalization, invokes his own special ritualistic celebration, with the aid of a little sack. The next few stanzas toast various poets and progressively involve larger and larger amounts of wine and greater and greater variation in their metrical schema. By the time the reader gets to stanza eight, in which Bacchus himself is toasted, he is quite willing to grant that, as the speaker in the "Welcome" claimed of Sack, "Thou mak'st me ayrie." It is interesting to note that even in these middle stanzas, where the various poets are being acknowledged, and where the persona is growing more "ayrie" by the line, it is actually the wine that is celebrated. Thus, each poet is presented in terms of a joke having something to do with the wine itself: it would make Homer see, and so forth.

With line 39, however, the poem comes to a sudden and forceful reversal. "But stay" puts an end to the "ayrieness," after the speaker has just promised a "flood" to Tibullus, and as he remembers Ovid's epitaph on that poet:

> Behold, *Tibullus* lies
>   Here burnt, whose smal return
> Of ashes, scarce suffice
>   To fill a little Urne.
>
> (ll. 41–44)

The thought is literally and metaphorically sobering, coming down so hard on the progressively "wanton" spirit of the preceding stanzas. The reader is suddenly jolted out of the dream world of the Rose into the very real world of mutability and death, of inevitability and utter waste. The "golden Pomp" of the ceremonial stasis gives way before the "funerall fire" of the temporal world.

In the final two stanzas, the speaker invokes poetry as the only means capable of transcending this funeral pyre:

> Trust to good Verses then;
>   They onely will aspire,
> When Pyramids, as men,
>   Are lost, i'th'funerall fire.

> And when all Bodies meet
>   In *Lethe* to be drown'd;
> Then onely Numbers sweet,
>   With endless life are crown'd.

(ll. 45–52)

The first of these stanzas is reminiscent of the Ovidian line which Herrick takes as an epigraph for his book. The second stanza repeats the idea in a new context. Poetry alone insures immortality, as the tenth stanza proves, because it is by way of verse that the speaker remembers Tibullus and his "text." And, of course, it is by way of verse that he remembers all the poets mentioned here. They are literally immortal. At the heat of the wine's influence, and at the suddenly sobering thought of death, the speaker comes to understand the ceremony of art itself.

The second group of courtly poems to be discussed in terms of the artistic ceremonial consists of dedicatory epigrams. The reason for placing these epigrams here rather than with the poems of the realistic persona is that while they purport to speak about actual people, they do not imitate or describe actual experience. They are, instead, another ritual of the court poet's activity and go quite beyond the suitor-patron dedications examined in Chapter III.

A relatively simple example of the type, but one which clearly indicates this persona's major concern, is "To the Earle of Westmerland" (H-112):

> WHen my date's done, and my gray age must die;
> Nurse up, great Lord, this my posterity:
> Weak though it be; long may it grow, and stand,
> Shor'd up by you, (*Brave Earle of Westmerland*).

The plea here is for poetic immortality: the poet's volume ("this my posterity") will last "long" if a benevolent and influential patron gives his support. The plea is conventional and is about as subservient as Herrick's persona allows himself to become. From this point on in the poems of this group, the need for a patron to assure longevity to the verse diminishes rapidly as poetry comes to stand more and more on its own. Still, the poem indicates the persona's main desire and in terms of the plea it is interesting to note that the only reference to the earl comes in a parenthetical expression. The poet is much more concerned with the immortality of his work than with complimenting a patron; to that extent, the reader's attention is also focused on the poetry itself rather than the figure to whom it is ostensibly addressed.

"To Mistresse Katherine Bradshaw, the lovely, that crowned him with Laurel" (H-224) not only defines the chief function of this dedicatory persona, but again shows Herrick's movement away from reliance on something or someone outside the poem to yield immortality to the verse:

> MY Muse in Meads has spent her many houres,
> Sitting, and sorting severall sorts of flowers,
> To make for others garlands; and to set
> On many a head here, many a Coronet:
> But, amongst All encircled here, not one
> Gave her a day of Coronation;
> Till you (sweet Mistresse) came and enterwove
> A *Laurel* for her, (ever young as love)
> You first of all crown'd her; she must of due,
> Render for that, a crowne of life to you.

Obviously, this persona sees one of his primary functions as the construction of poetic garlands, or poems in praise of certain individuals. There is a sense of refined pastoralism in the image of the first two lines which is not often found in dedicatory poems. But the main point of emphasis is in the final half-line: because Mistress Bradshaw has honored his poetry by her patronage, the poet will make a "crowne of life" for her. The crown here is another garland, but one significantly different from those mentioned in the opening lines. This is a garland of "life," an assurance of poetic immortality by means of this very poem.

Herrick makes a more forceful statement of the immortalizing power of the artistic ceremonial and of the mutability against which it is marshaled in "To his Honour'd friend, Sir Thomas Heale" (H-869):

> STand by the *Magick* of my powerfull Rhymes
> 'Gainst all the indignation of the Times.
> Age shall not wrong thee; or one jot abate
> Of thy both Great, and everlasting fate.
> While others perish, here's thy life decreed
> Because begot of my *Immortall* seed.

The "indignation of the Times" is, on one level, the transience, death, and putrefaction controlling all creation. The poem goes further than the preceding ones in the dogmatic self-assurance of its pronouncement. Contributing to this assurance is the use of the imperative in the first line. The rhymes are *"Magick"* because they are capable of transforming that which is mutable and hence under the control of time into that which is immutable, existing in a realm of artistic stasis. Thus, the *"Immortall* seed" of the concluding line refers to the art of poetry which grants Heale "eternal" friendship in, as Herrick's dedicatory persona elsewhere calls the *Hesperides*, "The Poets Endlesse-Kalendar." The whole poem illustrates the persona's confidence that "Age shall not wrong" his friend.

This dedicatory persona's conception of his volume provides an important insight into not only the nature of the artistic ceremonial, but the value of that ceremonial to the poet-creator. One working out of the concept occurs in "To the most learned, wise, and Arch-Antiquary, Master John Selden" (H-365):

> I Who have favour'd many, come to be
> Grac't (now at last) or glorifi'd by thee.
> Loe, I, the Lyrick Prophet, who have set

On many a head the Delphick Coronet,
Come unto thee for Laurell, having spent,
My wreaths on those, who little gave or lent.
Give me the *Daphne*, that the world may know it,
Whom they neglected, thou hast crown'd a Poet.
A City here of *Heroes* I have made,
Upon the rock, whose firm foundation laid,
Shall never shrink, where making thine abode,
Live thou a *Selden*, that's a Demi-god.

The poem begins in the same manner as the one to Katherine Bradshaw as the persona again talks about his function of setting "on many
a head the Delphick Coronet." But unlike the Bradshaw poem, this
one combines description with pleading as the poet asks Selden for his
authoritative approval. The subservient stance is closer to that in the
Westmerland poem. There is also an obvious element of complaint
in these first eight lines: those whom the "Lyrick Prophet" has made
immortal through his verse-compliments "little gave or lent" in return. Perhaps they did not even understand what it was he gave them.
The entire world seems to have neglected him as a poet. The plea and
the complaint suggest a basic insecurity on the part of the persona and
are hard to reconcile with the dogmatic assurance of the concluding
lines. The last four lines, in fact, seem to belong to a different poem
altogether. Possibly Herrick intends the incongruity in attitude to be
in some sense ironic: the poet need not worry about being neglected
and he need not sue Selden for approval—his poetry alone will accom-
plish all he desires.

The final lines of the poem allude to Jesus's description of Peter,
an allusion which is appropriate enough given this persona's proclivity
for discussing his "booke" in explicitly religious terms. The "rock"
here, of course, is poetry itself, on which the dedicatory and complimentary maker constructs "A City . . . of *Heroes*." And not only a
city, but an eternal city, "whose firm foundation laid,/ Shall never
shrink. . . ." Thus the persona is able to claim Selden as a "Demi-god"
—a mortal man, but an immortal, and hence godlike, one. The poet

no longer sues Selden for anything and in fact freely gives him yet another "Delphick Coronet." No longer is there any need to beg return, for the poet's task is complete; his realization that poetry alone insures its own immortality allows him to end on the self-confident and positive note.

As mentioned above, Herrick frequently refers to the *Hesperides* in these poems through the use of various epithets. Here the book is a city of heroes; elsewhere it is "my rich Plantation" (H-392), "the Poets Endlesse-Kalendar" (H-444), "this *white Temple* of my *Heroes*" (H-496), "The Generation of my Just" (H-664), "this eternall Coronet" (H-789), "My righteous race" (H-859), "My Just" (H-859), and "Fames *eternall Pedestall*" (H-1092), to name but a few. All of these epithets imply the immortalizing power of poetry and define a more encompassing ceremonial than has yet been suggested. The construction of this *"white Temple,"* the whole *Hesperides*, is a process of elevating, ordering, sanctifying, and suspending time. We, as readers, are asked to celebrate much more than the "heroes" making up that temple; we are asked to celebrate the poetry itself, the art of constructing the temple. Placed in the context of other poems in the same form, these dedicatory epigrams illustrate that however much Herrick might praise his individual patrons, he is more interested in what he can make of them than in any virtue or merit they have themselves. And what he makes, specifically, is a clearly defined realm of artistic stasis. Our response to the poetic ceremonial of any one poem is heightened by realization of the whole artistic rite in which it partakes and to which it contributes.

Two final dedicatory poems clarify the nature of this larger rite. The first is "To his Kinswoman, Mistresse Penelope Wheeler" (H-510):

> NExt is your lot (Faire) to be number'd one,
> Here, in my Book's Canonization:
> Late you come in; but you a Saint shall be,
> In Chiefe, in this Poetick Liturgie.

The most obvious feature of the epigram is Herrick's use of religious terminology to elevate Mistress Wheeler's character and to reinforce the immortality motif about which he is speaking. Even more than this, however, the terms help to establish and celebrate a kind of ritual quite distinct from Mistress Wheeler herself—that of poetry and the process of poetic creation. Simply to be included in this "Poetick Liturgie" is to be assured of "Canonization." The process of artistic creation sanctifies, in this sense, not only its subject matter, but itself as well.

"To his worthy Kinsman, Master Stephen Soame" (H-545) deals more fully with this type of imagery:

> NOr is my Number full, till I inscribe
> Thee sprightly *Soame*, one of my righteous Tribe:
> A Tribe of one Lip, Leven, and of One
> Civil Behaviour, and Religion.
> A stock of Saints; where ev'ry one doth weare
> A stole of white, (and Canonized here)
> Among which Holies, be Thou ever known,
> Brave Kinsman, markt out with the whiter stone:
> Which seals Thy Glorie; since I doe prefer
> Thee here in my eternall Calender.

"My righteous Tribe," "a stock of Saints," "my eternall Calender" —the poem is about the *Hesperides*, not about Soame; summary description of character here becomes description of the poet's volume. Soame is stabilized and defined only by the stock epithet of "saint"; even his "Civil Behaviour, and Religion" must be assumed. The point is that the poet is not concerned with individuals beyond their names. They function merely as catalysts which stimulate the act of poetic creation and which are subsumed in the artistic ceremonial once that act takes on a specific shape. It is the end product which most interests Herrick's persona—the sanctification of the artistic process by virtue of its capability to transform ordinary people into significant and immutable blocks of a towering and eternal edifice. In these two poems most of the bricks are made of religious terms which give the building an appearance of not only importance but sanctification. Still, it does not really matter what bricks are used, for the intention remains the same, and the manner of proceeding follows a deliberate plan: take the subject, elevate his importance, place him in a realm of ordered and controlled happenings, such as art, and the poem will yield an instant of stasis outside time and free from the ravages of transience and mutability. This is the nature of the artistic ceremonial of the dedicatory persona.

More can be said, however, about this persona's conception of himself. In many of these poems he calls himself a "lyrick prophet," or something similar, and though the emphasis in each poem is on the "prophet's" book, or temple, or city of heroes, it becomes evident that the persona is attempting to work out his own formula for going beyond time and the bounds that time places on his activities. It is interesting, therefore, that he rarely applies the poetic immortality which he so graciously lavishes on others to himself. This would hardly be politic, of course, in ostensibly dedicatory poems; they have little enough to do with the actual people involved as it is. But Herrick knows exactly what he is doing, for he must first of all establish poetry's capability to create the desired realm of stasis. He must demonstrate, that is, the ceremonial nature of the creative act and thereby its significance for human beings. With this group of poems, he accomplishes that goal and can go on in another series on poetry in general to assert that his "end" is the same as Mistress Wheeler's or Mr. Selden's, or that of any other recipient of his "eternal Coronet."

iii. THE REALISTIC VOICE

One small group of poems in which Herrick clarifies his relation to and his assumptions about poetry, especially its power to transcend the bounds of time, falls under the province of the realistic persona. As suggested in Chapter IV, the primary concern of this persona is to make definitive pronouncements, to turn what is possible into what actually is, to transmute private thought into public fact. In terms of the artistic ceremonial, this persona fulfills the necessary function of providing the theoretical foundation upon which the poet's conclusions about what art does must stand.[12] Once again these poems are written

12. When we see how carefully and methodically Herrick prepares for and

in the epigrammatic form, which is to say that they are not tentative explorations (or at least are not intended to be), but finalized, dogmatic assertions with which the reader is asked to agree. And it is important that he does agree, for the authority of the artistic persona and hence the validity of his art itself are at stake here.

"On his Booke" (H-1019) takes up the question of whether or not the poet is afforded the same immortality as the other "saints" of his "Temple":

> THe bound (almost) now of my book I see,
> But yet no end of those therein or me:
> Here we begin new life; while thousands quite
> Are lost, and theirs, in everlasting night.

"No end of those therein" gives the same assurance of poetic immortality found in the dedicatory poems; but the persona does not stop here, for the phrase "or me," falling as it does at the end of the line, underscores the point that he too achieves this desired end. "Here *we* begin new life" (my italics)—in terms of poetic immortality, the saints of the dedicatory poems and the author of those poems are at one.

The value of the artistic stasis is emphasized in "His desire" (H-1036), a poem which, to some readers, betrays Herrick's total lack of concern with events around him:

> GIve me a man that is not dull,
> When all the world with rifts is full:

---

defends his conclusions about the immortalizing power and value of art, it is impossible to accept Delattre's judgment on the poet's intentions in these poems: "Mais, et avec une inconséquente naïveté, il insiste sur le fait que cette vie immortelle est une faveur par lui seul conférée. C'est lui qui sera le grand prêtre du Temple de la Renommée (*Robert Herrick*, p. 143). Delattre later qualifies this assertion: "Cette confiance enthousiaste que Herrick met ainsi en la destinée de son oeuvre peut paraître indiscrète: elle est si naïve, comme si naturelle, qu'elle en semble moins outrecuidante. Avouons néanmoins que l'histoire littéraire offre peu d'exemples d'un auteur devoilant avec une telle nudité d'expression l'impudente idée qu'il se fait de son talent, tout en prétendant en faire hommage à autrui. Le *Exegi monumentum aere perennius* d'Horace paraît presque modeste en regard de cet orgueil que Herrick a si magnifiquement étendu à tout le 'collège' de ses protecteurs et de ses amis" (p. 146).

> But unamaz'd dares clearely sing,
> When as the roof's a tottering:
> And, though it falls, continues still
> Tickling the *Citterne* with his quill.

With those like Leon Mandel, who assume that Herrick is the "Last Elizabethan," the poem seems to agree. To those who would believe the poet oblivious of the changes being wrought in his world it gives a clear denial. Herrick does not display his disquietude as powerfully as, say, Donne does, but that does not mean he is unconcerned. His approach to these changes is fundamentally different. The persona of this poem is well aware that "the world with rifts is full" and that "the roof's a tottering"; after all, if the poem is as late chronologically as its place in the volume might imply (dangerous as that assumption might be), Herrick the royalist had, by this time, witnessed his world rapidly falling apart, had seen the king divested of all real control, and had himself been ousted from his parish. His response, however, is not to capitulate, but to "clearely sing." And if this "singing" reinvokes the old world view of the Elizabethans, it is simply because that view is ordered and reasonable; it provides authoritarian standards by which man can judge himself and his world. Strip away those standards by changing the world view and man has nowhere to turn, nothing to grasp. One of the poet's functions in this time of change, unrest, and doubt is to provide once more the older standards by dogmatically reinvoking the older view. He "sings" what is sure and certain, creating, with his "magical rhymes," an artistic stasis by which he and other men can see once more the order, the pattern, the essential reasonableness of things. For, as stressed from the beginning of this study, the ceremonial always presents a final view of reality, an integrated, controlled and ordered depiction of experience. Poetry not only "perpetuates the poet," but the age as well.

"To his Booke" (H-240) converts the traditional laurel crown, the wreath of poetic achievement, into an image of the poetry itself:

> THou art a plant sprung up to wither never,
> But like a Laurell, to grow green for ever.

In terms of the present group of epigrams, the most interesting feature of this poem is the persona's withdrawal: he treats only the eternity of the art work, not that of the creator. The thought is comparable to that in "Verses" (H-791), and emphasizes poetry's power to "outlive the bravest deeds of men."

"On himselfe" (H-554) gives an attempted dogmatic assertion by the artist-persona concerning his own end:

> SOme parts may perish; dye thou canst not all:
> The most of Thee shall scape the funerall.

The persona seems confident enough, but his hesitancy to state explicitly what part "shall scape" perhaps argues some lingering doubt. Presumably, the "part" could be either his soul or his poetry; that we recognize the greater validity of the second reading depends upon other statements in similar epigrams and upon our recollection of the epigraph to the volume itself: *"Effugient avidos Carmina nostra Rogos."* The poem attempts to present a dogmatic position regarding the achievement of the artist, but the ambiguity of the statement qualifies that dogmatism.

A second attempt at the same sort of assertion can be seen in "Upon himself" (H-366):

> THou shalt not All die; for while Love's fire shines
> Upon his Altar, men shall read thy lines;
> And learn'd Musicians shall to honour Herricks
> Fame, and his Name, both set, and sing his Lyricks.

The line "Thou shalt not All die" is essentially a paraphrase of the preceding poem, giving the same answer in more explicit terms: his verses will keep alive his "Fame, and his Name." But the persona is still not totally self-assured, for he needs to invoke lovers and the "learn'd Musicians" to first set his lyrics to music. The poems do not of themselves immortalize him. Once again the qualification weakens the dogmatic tone, even though love songs will surely continue to be sung.

In "On himselfe" (H-592), the artist returns to full self-assurance:

> LIve by thy Muse thou shalt; when others die
> Leaving no Fame to long Posterity:
> When Monarchies trans-shifted are, and gone;
> Here shall endure thy vast Dominion.

"Live by thy Muse thou shalt"—here there is no qualification, no ambiguity, no skirting of the issue. Poetry allows the poet to transcend death and "Times trans-shifting"; it raises him above the temporal to the "vast Dominion" of artistic stasis. Others may die, monarchies may crumble, but the poet and his creations continue secure and eternal. This is the ultimate statement of the epigrammatic speaker; his ceremonial of definitive pronouncement is completed. With the theoretical standard now securely established, Herrick can move on to the voice of the artist himself.

iv. THE ARTISTIC VOICE

The artistic ceremonial reaches its culmination in the voice of the poet-creator, the "singer" of the opening poem of the volume. The context for this voice is set in the Ovidian epigraph on the title page: "song alone escapes the greedy funeral pyre." In many ways, the *Hesperides* can be seen as a working out, in various ceremonial forms, of the truth of this assertion, or this promise. In the poems to be considered here, the artist is concerned to have his reader recognize exactly what sort of poetry he is writing. For this reason, "The Argument of his Book" properly belongs with this group, for it first introduces the special "singer" of the volume, the celebrator of the entire range of human experience. "When he would have his verses read" (H-8) continues the characterization of this speaker's songs:

> IN sober mornings, doe not thou reherse
> The holy incantation of a verse;
> But when that men have both well drunke, and fed,
> Let my Enchantments then be sung, or read.
> When Laurell spirts 'ith fire, and when the Hearth
> Smiles to it selfe, and guilds the roofe with mirth;

When up the *Thyrse* is rais'd, and when the sound
Of sacred *Orgies* flyes, A round, A round.
When the *Rose* raignes, and locks with ointments shine,
Let rigid *Cato* read these Lines of mine.

Although the persona here is quite close to the Bacchanalian celebrator discussed earlier, he is also much more. He begins by warning
against reading these "holy incantations" on "sober mornings";
rather, they must be read "when the *Rose* raignes" and songs to Bacchus fill the air. The poem is not a disclaimer of moral standards, as
some have suggested,[13] but an assertion that this is a special kind of
poetry and must be approached in a special way and a particular mood.
Herrick is establishing, in essence, a ritual of reading poetry, a rite
which in some ways contradicts the restriction of the poem's opening.
The relatively slow-moving lines, the religious imagery, the unique
celebratory setting, all suggest something quite different from the
Dionysian "orgies" to which the poem seemingly points. The "Orgy"
here is a "sacred" rite, not a wanton revel; there is a conscious sobriety
in the poem, as well as a morality. The point is that the poems are not
private meditations: they are public celebrations of various aspects of
reality. And because this type of ceremonial verse depends so heavily
upon the active response of its readers, it must be approached in the
proper ceremonial and celebratory frame of mind.

It must be emphasized that the establishment of this ritualistic pro-
cedure for reading the verse strongly argues the artist-persona's sense
of the significance of that verse. It is not to be taken lightly. These
are "holy incantations" and "sacred" songs: taken as a group, they
establish the liturgy of a unique religion of poetry. In many ways,
poetry *is* religion to this persona, and perhaps to Herrick as well. The
ceremonial here not only establishes a mood, but heightens the importance of the poetry and the creative act which affects it. The *Hesperides*
is to be approached by means of celebratory participation, by means of
ritual and religious devotion. Its verse is not simply a toy with which
to pass the time.

13. Swardson, *Poetry and the Fountain of Light*, pp. 41, 47–8.

In "His Poetrie his Pillar" (H-211) the artist-persona goes an important additional step in defining his verse:

1. ONely a little more
      I have to write,
      Then Ile give o're,
   And bid the world Good-night.

2. 'Tis but a flying minute,
      That I must stay,
      Or linger in it;
   And then I must away.

3. O time that cut'st down all!
      And scarce leav'st here
      Memoriall
   Of any men that were.

4. How many lye forgot
      In Vaults beneath?
      And piece-meale rot
   Without a fame in death?

5. Behold this living stone,
      I reare for me,
      Ne'r to be thrown
   Downe, envious Time by thee.

6. Pillars let some set up,
      (If so they please)
      Here is my hope,
   And my *Pyramides*.

The opening stanza is a good instance of the difficulty Herrick's poetry at times presents. In terms of paraphrasable meaning, the four lines say very little; emotionally, however, the stanza reveals much about the artist and his relationship to his work. The tone is subdued, re-signed, and sober; it is not quite melancholy, though it borders on that state. The real importance of the lines, and the tone, is the suggestion that writing poetry is a compulsion, a necessary act for the poet:

> ONely a little more
> *I have to write.* . . . (my italics)

We have not encountered this thought before in the volume, but it sheds a great deal of light (though a psychologically misty light perhaps) on the poet-poem association. The remainder of the lyric is essentially a working out of the reasons behind this compulsion.

Stanzas two through four present once more the poet's main stumbling block—the very reality, inevitability, and finality of death. Life is "but a flying minute" in which time "cut'st down all!" The speaker has descended, so to speak, into melancholy proper. And the major complaint is not merely that men die, but that they die "forgot." Time allows no memorial to stand, no fame to transcend the limits of death's end. The low point in the descending movement of the three stanzas comes in the final one, with the image of those who "piece-meale rot" in the grave. The emotional impact of "rot" is as strong as "Putrefaction" in the epigram of that title. As is usually the case with this sort of descent, however, the downward movement prepares for a corresponding ascent and the persona ends, in the final two stanzas, on a more hopeful note. "This living stone," this poem, is "Ne'r to be thrown/ Downe" by "envious Time." This "Pyramid" (presumably the shape of each stanza is meant to suggest a pillar) will last far beyond the bounds of the poet's own life. "Here is [his] hope."

The reader is now in a position to understand the full implications of the opening stanza. In a world of oppressively certain mutability, of transience and death, the writing of poetry becomes a compulsive and necessary act if the artist is to have any hope of transcending the limits of his own temporal existence.[14] Furthermore, the term "compulsive"

14. Cf. Haydn's assertion that "it seems as though they [the Elizabethan poets] *felt a defiant need* to deny the very truth that so often overshadowed their delight in the world of physical experience—the knowledge that it must end, that the blossoms had to die and the shadows slip away [my italics]" (*The Counter-Renaissance*, p. 365). See also his discussion of the "Metaphysical Ache"—the need, in turn, to transcend the mutable limits which they insistently emphasized (pp. 367–73).

implies more than first assumed. The poet, because he sees more clearly the true nature of his experience, also feels more acutely the lesson of that experience:

> PUtrefaction is the end,
> Of all that Nature doth entend.

But man cannot live without hope, which poetry provides. Only by an active participation in the ceremony of art, in the "singing" of experiences in order to create an "artifice of eternity," can the poet find any sort of fulfillment. That "artifice" is the cardinal end of the artistic ceremonial.

One of the most difficult poems in the *Hesperides*, "His Winding-sheet" (H-515), presents another view of the relationship between the poet and his poem. In order to understand this poem completely, however, it is first necessary to glance briefly at "Poetry perpetuates the Poet" (H-794):

> HEre I my selfe might likewise die,
> And utterly forgotten lye,
> But that eternall Poetrie
> Repullulation gives me here
> Unto the thirtieth thousand yeere,
> When all now dead shall re-appeare.

The poem presents a unique thought in the volume and a unique combination of "immortalities." Poetry, the persona claims, serves as a kind of eternal bridge connecting the poet's earthly life and his afterlife in the "great Platonick yeere." The latter image is synthesized, by means of the final line, with the Judaic-Christian Last Judgment. The persona can rest assured that at the end of the temporal cycle, everything will return to its original form and he and the rest of the dead will once more return to life, this time to an eternal life. Until this "Platonick" year arrives, however, he is also assured of a "temporary" immortality by means of his verse. In terms of the poems we have been examining in this chapter, the concept is totally original, even somewhat startling in its relegating of poetic immortality to a secondary, almost stop-gap position. But the assurance of poetic immortality is at least still present. In "His Winding-sheet" it is not.

COme thou, who art the Wine, and wit
    Of all I've writ:
The Grace, the Glorie, and the best
    Piece of the rest.
Thou art of what I did intend
    The All, and End.
And what was made, was made to meet
    Thee, thee my sheet.
Come then, and be to my chast side
    Both Bed, and Bride.
We two (as Reliques left) will have
    One Rest, one Grave.
And, hugging close, we will not feare
    Lust entring here:
Where all Desires are dead, or cold
    As is the mould:
And all Affections are forgot,
    Or Trouble not.
Here, here the Slaves and Pris'ners be
    From Shackles free:
And weeping Widowes long opprest
    Doe here find rest.
The wronged Client ends his Lawes
    Here, and his Cause.
Here those long suits of Chancery lie
    Quiet, or die:
And all Star-chamber-Bils doe cease,
    Or hold their peace.
Here needs no Court for our Request,
    Where all are best;
All wise; all equall; and all just
    Alike i'th'dust.

> Nor need we here to feare the frowne
>   Of Court, or Crown.
> *Where Fortune bears no sway o're things,*
>   *There all are Kings.*
> In this securer place we'l keep,
>   As lull'd asleep;
> Or for a little time we'l lye,
>   As Robes laid by;
> To be another day re-worne,
>   Turn'd, but not torn:
> Or like old Testaments ingrost,
>   Lockt up, not lost:
> And for a while lye here conceal'd,
>   To be reveal'd
> Next, at that great Platonick yeere,
>   And then meet here.

The artist-persona begins by invoking his poetry (or perhaps this particular poem) as the best thing he has done, the "End" toward which all his labor has been directed. Furthermore, his poetry "was made to meet/ Thee, thee my sheet." It is like a shroud in that it is a preparation for death, a way of getting ready to die. Poetry is both the literal "sheet" on which he fulfills his function as a creator and the fulfillment of that function: it is the means and the end, the "Bed, and the Bride." But the opening invocation omits any reference to an immortality achieved through the creative process. Rather, it is simply a definition of the poet in terms of his poetry, or at least in terms of the activity of writing poetry.[15]

The second section of the poem (ll. 11–18) is a Marvellian description of the grave, where all emotions and desires hang, for a time, suspended. The persona's poetry will remain here with him; it does

15. It may be objected that the opening section of the poem is addressed to a literal winding sheet and that, as one of the readers of this manuscript has suggested, the sheet is seen as "a *momento mori*—the object to which Life and Poetry both ultimately incline—or decline." I do not think our readings here are mutually exclusive.

not seem to have any life of its own. This is an astonishing inversion of all we have been led to expect in these poems, for poetry here provides no essential transcendence and does not itself escape the finality and obscurity of death—or at least this is what the poem seems to be saying.

Lines 19–36 present a further description of the grave, one in which the tone alters from somber seriousness to something closer to sarcasm and even cynicism directed at the natural condition of man. All the injustices of life will be equalized in death: "All wise; all equall; and all just/ Alike i'th'dust." Here *"Fortune bears no sway"*; all is in a stasis beyond the control of "envious Time." It is, for the persona, a "securer place," in which there are no desires, no troubles, no enjoyment even—just the peace of "sleep."

In the final twelve lines Herrick returns to the image of the "great Platonick yeere" when all shall "meet here" once more. The reference is to some kind of immortality, although it is far less specific than the allusion in "Poetry perpetuates the Poet." Regardless of the exact nature of the immortality anticipated, it *is* expected and that expectation brings to the final lines an element of hope. The poem is finally neither melancholy nor sad; rather, it evokes a quality of serene acceptance and almost, though not quite, celebratory anticipation. The sensation is vague, admittedly, because the statement in which it is shrouded is vague, but it is there nonetheless.

As opposed to most of the poems examined in this chapter, "His Winding-sheet" does not make claims of transcendence. In this sense, its ceremonial nature is not quite the same as the others', even though it is still ceremonial. All the poems in which the speaker posits the eternity of poetry indicate one significant fact—the finality with which the poet apprehends death necessitates the attempt on his part to go beyond that finality, forces him, that is, to create a moment of artistic stasis in which death is rendered as somehow more meaningful than simply the end of the natural process. If he is successful in the attempt, then it is assumed he will be "ready" in a sense for death. He will have created the means of his own transcendence. In this way, all of the poems are "preparations" for death, are ceremonies of art

which, like his shroud, must be completed before he is ready to accede
to death: "His Winding-sheet" is no different in this respect, for the
treatment in ceremonial and poetic terms of the grave and of the final
anticipated release from that grave is once more a "preparation" for
dying. The difference between this poem and the others is that the
persona explicitly shows here that he is himself conscious of the "preparative" act, that he recognizes the "compulsion" of his own cre-
ativity. And by displaying that consciousness, he directs his readers, not
to the literal poem itself, but to the artistic motivation behind it. It
is the assurance that the ceremony of artistic creation yields that
makes it possible for the poet-persona to accept his "end," his literal
"Winding-street."[16]

To return to the more typical "preparative" poems, we may look
briefly at one final example, the penultimate poem of the *Hesperides*,
"The pillar of Fame" (H-1129):

> FAmes pillar here, at last, we set,
> Out-during *Marble*, *Brasse*, or *Jet*,
>> Charm'd and enchanted so,
>> As to withstand the blow
>>> Of   overthrow :
>>> Nor shall the seas,
>>> O r   O u t r a g e s
>>> Of storms orebear
>>> What we up-rear,
>>> Tho Kingdoms fal,
>> This   pillar   never   shall
>> Decline or waste at all;
> But stand for ever by his owne
> Firme and well fixt foundation.

16. Whitaker claims that the poem suggests a "more insidious temptation to
use the imaginative world as mere escape" ("Herrick and the Fruits of the
Garden," p. 28). But the speaker never denies the fact of his own death. How,
then, is he escaping? In fact, if one were arguing on these terms alone, it would
seem that this poem is far less "escapist" than any of those discussed in this chapter.

The poem gives the same assured belief in the immortality of verse seen in the companion piece, "His Poetrie his Pillar." The only addition to this line of thought is the strong assertion that the poetry will stand "by his *owne*/ Firm and well fixt foundation" (my italics). Of more interest, however, is the shape of the poem, which visually mirrors the pillar of its title. We normally associate this device almost exclusively with George Herbert, but Herrick too makes use of it on several occasions.[17] Structurally, the device works well here as the dogmatic assertions of the strengths of poetry occupy the longer lines at the top and bottom of the pillar, thereby bounding and enclosing the destructive elements of time and mutability occupying the shorter middle lines. Likewise, the "foundation" of the poem's idea comes structurally at the bottom of the visual image. Finally, the symmetry of the design supports both the assertion of artistic control and the emotional stability of the tone.[18]

There is one other interesting feature here, a kind of visual pun, for although the shape of the poem is obviously intended to represent a pillar, it also represents the form of a traditional classical altar, as a glance at Herbert's "The Altar" will indicate. This "pun" suggests much about the poetry itself, things which have been stressed in the course of this study—its essentially religious nature, the ritualistic character of its ceremonial mode, and so on. The creation of the artistic stasis is, for this persona, a "religious" act. On the altar of poetry he celebrates and pays homage to his experience and his art. And on the altar of poetry, as two preceding poems—"The mount of the Muses" (H-1123) and "On Himselfe" (H-1128)—suggest,

17. See Kimmey's limited but helpful discussion of Herrick's use of this kind of poem in "Order and Form in Herrick's *Hesperides*," pp. 259–68; Patrick also notes the importance of shapes in Herrick's poetry in his introductory comments to the Norton edition of his *Complete Poetry*.

18. See Puttenham's discussion of the meaning of the pillar shape in the *Arte of English Poesie*: "The Pillar is a figure among all the rest of the Geometricall most beawtifull, in respect that he is tall and vpright and of one bignesse from bottom to the toppe. In Architecture he is considered with two accessarie parts, a pedestall or base, and a chapter or head; the body is the shaft. By this figure is signified stay, support, rest, state, and magnificence" (Smith, *Elizabethan Critical Essays*, II, 100–1).

his icon will remain, fixed, permanent, a living memorial to the god of art and ceremony.

v. THE COMPLETED CEREMONIAL

It is not necessary to regard every poem in the *Hesperides* as ceremonial to see that celebration is the governing intention behind most of them and that the poetic ceremonial is the shaping principle through which that intent is most often actualized. By transforming literal and private actions into significant, public rituals, Herrick's poems continually isolate and re-present, in heightened and ordered form, key moments of human experience. By freeing these moments from temporal control, the poet leads us to an understanding of what each involves. Surely one measure of his success in demonstrating how meaningful these ritual moments are is the freedom and the ease with which we, as readers, can commit ourselves to the constructed rites.

To a large extent, however, the true success of the *Hesperides* lies not with individual poems. There are, certainly, some poems here as fine in their way as any in the century—"Corinna," "Delight in Disorder," "The Night-piece, to Julia," "The Argument," the "Sack" poems, and so on—but it is a feeling of joy and festivity, even of a kind of free abandonment to the vitality of communal impulses, which is evoked by a reading of the volume as a whole. The artistic stasis which Herrick achieves within the limits of his poetical garden does in fact go far beyond the mutability concerns giving rise to the book. In this way Herrick raises larger questions about the act of creative writing itself and the function of poetry within the framework of human experience.

To pursue this line of thought but one step further, it is possible perhaps to see the *Hesperides* as a kind of poetical dialectic. By using different personae, Herrick is able to pit one ceremonial approach to existence against another, to show that each is significant on its own terms and within its own limits, and to demonstrate that the *poetic* ceremonial, the rite of artistic or imaginative creation, is one means of actualizing all these approaches simultaneously. Herrick's own consciousness of the artistic rite in which he is engaged gives ultimate meaning to the volume that rite produces. The British novelist-poet-critic, Paul West, in a book entitled *The Wine of Absurdity*, acutely summarizes in abstract form this final level of meaning:

All man can do is to *re*-create himself, each within his own limits, taking his mystique where he finds it without expecting morals from it, being as rational as he can . . . , and acting with as full a sense of responsibility as he can manage in a world where he is always in motion. To remain a coherent person entails always an effort of imagination, for imagination is the only means we have of going beyond minimal awareness. To be ourselves is to deal with ourselves on the move between inexplicable birth and inexplicable death; and imagination, whether we call it mystique or reason or action [or the construction of poetic rituals], is the only weapon we have against death.[19]

Robert Herrick may not ultimately be a "Great Poet" in Eliot's sense of the term, but his achievement is none the less because of that. To participate in his poetic ceremonial fully and consciously is to understand how far the creative act may take us.

19. West, *The Wine of Absurdity* (University Park, 1966), pp. 248–49.

INDEX

41, 179; epitaph, 11, 68, 112, 143–
44, 151–63; epithalamium, 104–
06; fairy poem, 12, 23, 67–68;
game lyric, 74, 93–95; immortality
lyric, 103–04, 107–08, 172–78; impossibilities lyric, 73, 84, 86, 89–
91, 169; paradoxical encomium,
168–69; passionate-shepherd lyric,
54–55, 65, 119; parting verse, 74,
95–96; Petrarchan love-lyric, 74–
76, 84–85, 168; praise-of-grotesque
lyric, 88; protestation, 74, 84–91;
sonnet, 6–8; verse-compliment, 70,
74, 76–84; 97, 106, 149, 168, 175
Gilbert, Allan H., 18
Godolphin, Sidney, 69
Gordon, D. J., 11, 12
Green, Thomas, 104
Gosse, Edmund, 68, 80, 109

Happy life, theme of, *see* Pastoral
motifs
Hardison, O. B., 152
Haydn, Hiram, 10, 27, 45, 185
Her Bed (H-348), 83–84
Herbert, George, 140, 191
Hesperides: as an artistic world, 8,
174–78; humor (or wit), 26, 30,
63, 86–89, 93, 115–24, 140, 146,
150, 169–70; juxtaposition of
genres, 37, 119, 122, 192; music
and meter, 26, 42, 44, 72, 86–87,
139–40, 160, 171, 183; order, 37,
50, 119, 122, 157, 180, 192; prov-
erbs and *sententiae*, 37, 39, 92–93,
115, 125–26, 131; realism versus
idyllic, 63, 110, 113–14, 120, 125,
136, 140; religious imagery, 3, 31,
57–58, 60–62, 66, 73, 77, 86, 92,
103, 117, 119, 129–30, 132, 144,
148–49, 159, 162–63, 175–77, 183,
191–92; royalism, 101–02, 134–
36; satire, 110, 112, 115–17, 121–
25; tone as qualifying note, 26, 29–
30, 42, 49, 64–65, 132, 146, 175,
181; vulgarity, 109, 115, 120–25;
see also Genres *and* Personae
Heywood, John, 120
Hibbard, G. R., 31
Highet, Gilbert, 27
Hirsh, Edward L., 7

His content in the Country (H-552),
24, 26–28, 29, 30, 33
His desire (H-1036), 179–80
His embalming to Julia (H-327),
148–49, 155
His fare-well to Sack (H-128), 168–
69, 192
His Grange, or private wealth (H-
724), 24, 28–30, 33
*His Lachrimae or Mirth, turn'd to
mourning* (H-371), 72, 73
His own Epitaph (H-617), 159
*His parting from Mistresse Dorothy
Keneday* (H-122), 95
His Poetrie his Pillar (H-211), 184–
86, 191
His Protestation to Perilla (H-154),
84, 89–90
His returne to London (H-713), 72,
73
His sailing from Julia (H-35), 95
His Winding-sheet (H-515), 186–90
Hock-cart, The (H-250), 12, 14, 23,
46–50, 51, 67
Horace, 19, 20, 22, 27, 31, 165–66

Ill Government (H-536), 135–36
Immortality, *see* Poetic immortality
Immortality lyric, *see* Genres
Impossibilities lyric, *see* Genres
Impossibilities to his friend (H-198),
90–91
In the darke none dainty (H-586),
88–89
Ironic mode, 9, 13

Jenkins, Paul R., 20, 32
Jonson, Ben, 12, 20, 31, 68, 71, 86,
111, 117, 121, 129, 164; *see also*
Tribe of Ben
Julia's Petticoat (H-175), 81–83

Kimmey, John, 5, 30, 37, 110, 121–
23, 127, 139, 191

Langer, Susanne K., 5, 16
Large Bounds doe but bury us (H-
542), 129
Leavis, F. R., 16
Lewis, C. S., 11
Lodge, Thomas, 69, 89